Bearing Witness

Poetry by Teachers about Teaching

Edited by
MARGARET HATCHER

Zephyr Press
Tucson, Arizona

Editorial Review Board

Bearing Witness: Poetry by Teachers about Teaching
© 2002 by Margaret Hatcher

Professional Growth

Printed in the United States of America

ISBN: 1-56976-130-2

Developmental & Copy Editing: Jenny Flynn
Design & Production: Dan Miedaner
Cover: Dan Miedaner

Published by:
Zephyr Press
P.O. Box 66006
Tucson, Arizona 85728-6006
800-232-2187
www.zephyrpress.com
www.i-home-school.com

Library of Congress Cataloging-in-Publication Data

Bearing witness : poetry by teachers about teaching / Margaret Hatcher, editor.
    p. cm.
  Includes index.
  ISBN 1-56976-130-2 (alk. paper)
   1. Teachers' writings, American. 2. American poetry—20th century. 3. Education—Poetry. 4. Teaching—Poetry. 5. Schools—Poetry. I. Hatcher, Margaret.

PS591.T4 B43 2002
811'.5080355—dc21
                                         2001022031

⌒ ACKNOWLEDGMENTS ⌒

I wish to express my sincere appreciation and gratitude and to acknowledge the contributions made to this book by the following:

- ⌒ To each and every teacher/poet who so generously and vulnerably submitted your poetry for this book. I am honored and humbled by your poems. If I could have, I would have used them all.

- ⌒ To all of my teachers, from elementary school through my doctoral studies, as well as those of you such as Angeles Arrien who have served as teachers and mentors of my growth as an adult—thank you not only for touching and shaping my life in profound ways, but for making a difference in the world by touching the lives of thousands of others.

- ⌒ To my many students over four decades of serving as an educator; you have been among my most inspiring and powerful teachers.

- ⌒ To my parents, both caring and outstanding educators for forty years, who gifted me with the legacy of a passion for learning, educational excellence, integrity, and compassion.

- ⌒ To my many colleagues and friends who are teachers; you are my heroines and heroes. You have inspired, informed, enlarged, and supported me in my growth and understanding of our profession.

- ⌒ To Lola Bonner, who was the teacher who served as the catalyst for changing my life by seeing a spirit and a potential in me that I could not see in myself at the time. Thank you for your subtle and tender care, support, encouragement, and belief in me.

- ⌒ To my insightful and dedicated editorial review board, who saw me through the early times with encouragement and support: Dr. Peggy Raines, Dr. Sally M. Oran, Emilie Rodger, Martha Brady, and Dr. Pat Wall—all ex-public school teachers, gifted writers, and highly respected and talented teacher education colleagues at Northern Arizona University in Flagstaff, Arizona. Thank you for your support, your encouragement of and belief in this project, your hours of time and effort put into reading the poems and agonizing over the cuts we had to make, and your integrity of discernment and judgment of the literary merit of the poems.

- ⌒ To Zephyr Press for recognizing and valuing the worth of this project, and especially to Jenny Flynn, developmental editor, for her unceasing belief in the project, her patience with me, her enthusiasm, and her consistently prompt, open, and candid communication throughout the project.

- ⌒ And, perhaps most importantly, to my best friend, educational peer/colleague and partner Peggy, whose integrity and nurturing continues to deepen and change me and whose book this is as much as mine.

CONTENTS

PREFACE

I n a tribute to one of his teachers, John Steinbeck recounted his still-vivid
memory of a powerful teacher in his life, recalling how "she breathed curiosity
into us so that each morning we came to her class carrying new truths, new
facts, new ideas, cupped and shielded in our hands like captured fireflies." He
described his sadness when she was no longer his teacher, but noted that "the
light did not go out. She had written her signature upon us; the literature of the
teacher who writes on children's minds." Finally, he observed: "I have had many
teachers who taught me soon forgotten things; but only a few like her who created
in me a new direction, a new hunger, a new attitude. I suppose to a large extent I
am the unsigned manuscript of that teacher. What deathless power lies in the
hands of such a person."

Indeed, each of us is an unsigned manuscript of our teachers. And, like Steinbeck,
each of us carries within us a vibrant, still-living legacy of our teachers. We can
recall their faces and their names years and decades after they touched our lives,
and we can tell colorful, passionate, detailed, and specific stories about them as if
these memories happened to us only yesterday. Some of those memories are inspiring,
filled with love, respect, humor, and awe, and some are filled with pain, humiliation,
and anger. No, not one of us would deny the life-changing power held in the
hands of teachers. Teachers indeed do touch and shape our future.

Teachers are my personal heroes and heroines, not only because of their impact
in touching the minds, hearts, lives, potential, and dreams of their students, but
also because they are intelligent, knowing, caring, curious, selfless people. Day
after day, year after year, teachers humbly and graciously perform difficult and
demanding work with huge responsibilities and even greater impact, often while
receiving few extrinsic rewards and little recognition. James Hobbs, a highly loved
and respected teacher in Colorado, points out that "teachers hold in their hands
the lights to the world," yet unfortunately, in today's culture, teachers are among
the most maligned, criticized, underpaid, and undervalued of all professionals.
Because of this fact, I have felt compelled to edit this book.

My purpose in gathering together the poems in this anthology is to create a
positive, inspirational, yet realistic picture of teachers and the very challenging
and complex contexts within which they weave their magic in their students'
lives and make endless contributions to our world. I want to reveal, through teachers'
own voices and personal points of view, the insight, intelligence, heart, complexity,
compassion, human goodness, and magnificence of teachers. I want to show from

the inside out how teachers think and feel about teaching, learning, and their students. And lastly, I want to offer a glimpse of teachers' inner lives, how they themselves learn and grow as persons, and something of the context in which they must teach and in which they serve their profession, communities, and world.

The poetry included in this book comes from teachers all over this country and from all levels of our educational system; they are poems from teachers in K–12 schools and community colleges and universities. Some of the poems have been published elsewhere, but many have never been published before. Some of the poems were written years ago, and some were created for this anthology. However, without exception, these poems reveal the articulate, powerful, profound, and authentic voices of teachers. These voices must be heard so that, without the clamor of educational debate, political agendas, and pedagogical jargon, we may bear witness to and see into the minds and hearts of teachers. These poems bear witness to teachers' commitment to, love of, and context of teaching and learning. In addition, they bear witness to teachers' own inner lives, personal growth and learning, and belief in students' selfhood, well-being, and potential.

The poems collected in this anthology were selected from literally thousands of poems. As editor, my selection process was a simple one: I sent out the call for poems by teachers through my own personal network of educators, teaching organizations, conferences and journals for educators, and teachers' groups such as the national writing project networks. I read and reread more than two thousand poems, cutting to a list of approximately five hundred. Next, I submitted the poems to my editorial review board, which was composed of five educational colleagues who are also teachers, excellent writers, and lovers of poetry.

While all final choices were my responsibility, the board gave outstandingly perceptive and candid advice in assisting me to select the best mix of poems for the book. We had to eliminate literally hundreds of fine poems from the collection due to considerations of density and length of the book, but hopefully this will be only the first volume in a series of anthologies of poetry by teachers.

These are not "sweet or sappy" poems or "schmaltzy tributes" to teachers. However, I do believe them to be quite moving, because they deal with the realities and complexities of teachers' work and lives, as well as the realities of teachers' relationships with students. The criteria used in the selection of the poetry included in the collection were:

෴ best fit with the book's vision and themes

෴ power and impact of the poem's message

෴ quality, use, vividness, and specificity of detail, symbol, and image

෴ a sense of "reality"

෴ effectiveness of the poet's voice, style, and structure

෴ consistency of point of view

ﾠ a strong sense of heart and meaning about teachers and teaching

ﾠ originality and creativity

When I was an aspiring poet at the Breadloaf Writing Institute in Vermont, one of the poets-in-residence encouraged us again and again to "notice consciously and name specifically," stressing that there is great power in this very simple act. Over the years, I have come to believe that he was absolutely correct. To notice consciously means to be totally present, in the moment, awake and alive to all that is around us and in us. To name specifically is to dare telling the truth of our experience and observations without blame, judgment, excuse, or equivocation. And when we are able to perform this daring act of noticing and naming, we write our best poems, poems that leave us silent and wordless. I believe this collection has many such poems that add to our respect, alter our images, inform our minds, enlarge our spirits, and enhance our understanding and appreciation of teachers. In these poems, we sense toughness as well as tenderness, despair as well as hope and passion, fatigue as well as joy, humor as well as frustration, and the sacred grace as well as the humanity of teachers. As we read their poetry, we sense that these teachers claim their own power, their own identities, and their own humanity. And in reading these poems, they challenge us, too, to claim our own humanity, compassion, grace, hope, passion, and joy.

This is a book not only for teachers, but for everyone. It is for anyone who has ever had a teacher who made a difference in his or her life, for students and their parents, for friends and family of teachers, and for administrators and school-board members. It is for all of us who want to acknowledge, celebrate, and bear witness to the teachers in our lives. ﾠ

Teachers' Poetry about

TEACHING

INTRODUCTION

Teachers' Poetry about Teaching
Sally M. Oran

i am a continuance
of blue sky
i am the throat
of the sandia mountains
a night wind woman
who burns
with every breath
she takes
—Joy Harjo

I have always been fascinated with transitions. Edges of ecosystems transform life into mystical and diverse forms. Ocean energies move through the surf to enter tidal pools that feed my imagination. The science teacher in me knows that forest against field, sagebrush with juniper, cattails with caddis flies, and hail on high mesas all nurse nature's web. The biodiversity that marks the boundaries of these entwined environments holds treasures and mysteries that stir my energy, my questions, and my understanding. What more could anyone want than to stand in the wash of wonder?

I have been privileged to know this wonder in the several places where I have lived. I have come to seek it as a requirement for any residence or recreation. I was a child of the city, the nation's capital, who befriended stately sycamores that marched along granite curbs and shed the bark of miniature canoes near bus stops. In the hills of Tennessee I recognized the yearly migrations of birds and how different species echoed the health and variety of my home woods, streams, swamps, and fields. In the Southwest, where I now live, I inhale the warm breath of ponderosas that grow at seven thousand feet, and I trace their spires to the stars. This is the way I search for the essential intersections between me and the children I teach: alert for the signposts of our mutual surprise, the edges of our energy, the sites where our questions queue to fuel our shared wonder.

The environment at these intersections, edges, and transition sites can be harsh with changes and contrasts. In my classroom these transitions are charged shadows where life's magic connects with understanding. Fine teachers know that both teaching and learning require the freedom to question and defy established answers with new data. Great teachers practice such freedom by creating classrooms where alternative solutions are accepted and expected. _Here no!_ collides with _Yes, where?_ entreats _Here_ and _Why?_ interrogates _Because._ Here the breakers of ego crash to energize the idea zone; the fires of the mind rage to restore life and protocols decay to feed knowledge. Here is where teachers are learners and students guide curricula with their own inherent knowledge. Real classrooms are safe havens for every voice, every language, every question, and every dream. They are the very homes of hope.

In this section of this anthology, you will read accounts of teachers who describe the edges of teaching and learning, the intersections of hope and life in their classrooms. Listen as their words explore the smooth paths and rocky circuits of daily interactions with students. There are fine days with sunny skies and gentle breezes; there are also storms and high seas and blowing sand that stings. There is the painful yet practical response of a teacher who realizes the picnic basket beside a student's desk holds a hungry infant in "No Picnic." There is the expectancy of a teacher's rebirth to learning in "New Class," and there is the glory of remembering a teacher who dared to demonstrate the energy of love in "A Charm in His Arms." Teacher-poets are caught in the turnstile of their own lives as in "On My First Year of Teaching" and at the crossroads of curricula and current events in "Undivided Attention." And within the pages of this section echo the pulses of teachers who tackle the terrible and contemplate the unmentionable as in "On Wiesel's _Night_" and "Telling My Sister How I Taught a Lesson on Child Abuse."

These poems create images that evidence the interface between lives and events that occur daily in classrooms. As you read on, celebrate the seasons of truthfulness and courage these poets share about life and learning, teaching, and hope. ✒

CONTENTS OF THIS SECTION

CONTENTS OF THIS SECTION *(continued)*

Composition

—for Jeff Arnett

Charles Atkinson

". . . the light that shines in all things."

Framed across the courtyard, in a classroom window,
a man—a teacher—stares out through sheeting rain.
I know him: We do the same work. Is it the weather
or desperation? He's asked them to confide in their journals,
urgent letters on the board—WHERE IS YOUR LIGHT?

They've pulled around the table, heads bowed; silent
bark of a winter cold. Some draw their shoulders
around the page; a few tilt back, feet propped on the table;
their wet boots shine. Are they printing at the top:
Thursday, February 28—Where is my light?

He's changed the rules; how to trust him? No one looks up:
frowns, a stocking cap low and noncommittal, wet slicker
tossed aside. *What does he want?* This is heart's country:
KEEP OUT. He's bent over a journal of his own
as if sheer effort might wake them into their lives.

Time must be up—the books riffle shut. He took a chance—
write the truth for once. Now the formal lesson, in chalk:
thesis statement, topic sentence, the semicolon's use.
I cheer across the courtyard, but it's lost in the downspout's
clang, so I turn to a new page and begin: *Framed across . . .* ❧

What Teachers Make

Taylor Mali

He says the problem with teachers is "What's a kid going to learn
from someone who decided his best option in life was to become a teacher?"
He reminds the other dinner guests that it's true what they say about teachers:
Those who can, do; those who can't, teach.

I decide to bite my tongue instead of his
and resist the temptation to remind the dinner guests
that it's also true what they say about lawyers.

Because we're eating, after all, and this is polite company.
"I mean, you're a teacher," he says.
"Be honest. What do you make?"

And I wish he hadn't done that
(asked me to be honest)
because, you see, I have a policy
about honesty and ass-kicking:
if you ask for it, I have to let you have it.

You want to know what I make?

I make kids work harder than they ever thought they could.
I can make a C+ feel like a Congressional Medal of Honor
and an A– feel like a slap in the face.
How dare you waste my time with anything less than your very best.

I make kids sit through 40 minutes of study hall
In absolute silence. No, you may not work in groups.
No, you may not ask a question.
Why won't I let you get a drink of water?
Because you're not thirsty, you're bored, that's why.

I make parents tremble in fear when I call home:
I hope I haven't called at a bad time,
I just wanted to talk to you about something Billy said today.

Billy said, "Leave the kid alone. I still cry sometimes, don't you?"
And it was the noblest act of courage I have ever seen.

I make parents see their children for who they are
and what they can be.

You want to know what I make?

I make kids wonder.
I make them question.
I make them criticize.
I make them apologize and mean it.
I make them write.
I make them read, read, read.
I make them spell definitely beautiful, definitely beautiful, definitely beautiful
over and over and over again until they will never misspell
either one of those words again.
I make them show all their work in math.
And hide it on their final drafts in English.
I make them understand that if you got this (brains)
then you follow this (heart) and if someone tries to judge you
by what you make, you give them this (the finger).

Let me break it down for you, so you know what I say is true:
I make a goddamn difference! What about you? ᶘ

A Morning Like This

Camille Balaban

if there can be a morning like this
when I sip coffee
with my nose inches from
a branch of lilac
sitting carelessly in an old ice bucket
on the kitchen table
and if the lavender scent
can distract me from the morning news
long enough for me to wonder
how those tiny flowerets
ever knew enough to bunch together
on a tough branch surrounded by
bright green leaves almost large enough
to overpower their fragrance

then, I guess I will live
beyond the glaring headlines
which tell of a full school bus
smashing into a car
containing five other students
from the same school
killing one young girl
who sat next to the driver

and, though lilacs won't bring back life
or ease the pain of the bus driver
a woman, who, only last year
buried her teenaged son,
a boy who had chosen not to live,
these purple buds
that open suddenly into lacy trumpets
soften, for me, the memory of that same boy
sitting in my class
taunting me with his impish ways

leaving me to wonder forever
why his days were so heavy
when, if he had looked, he might have seen
lilacs in bloom, robins in a green field,
and the fact that tentative mornings
always offer enough possibility
to help us walk gently
through another day. 🍂

Teacher Me Sweet

C. Drew Lamm

Some September I'm going to have me a teacher so
sweet. That teacher's going to smile on me. When I
come to school she'll be glad. She'll dig deep into
my soul and mine diamonds.

She'll smile with her apple-seed eyes and say, "This
one's so sweet. I'm going to take good care."

And she will.

She'll search me through my eyes. She'll see a
smooth lake waiting for a ripple, and she'll see
silver waiting to be shined.
She'll open her arms, and keep them there all year.

She'll talk liquid drops, smooth and slow. I won't
drown in her words.

And she'll smile when I talk and ask questions she
really wants to know.

If I'm confused in my head and hurting from so
much thinking, she'll put her arm around me and
say, "Breathe sweet."

And if I come to school so mad because my life
hurts and nobody ever listens to me,

she'll listen.

She'll listen so sweet, like the sky so wide and deep.
She'll listen like the air at twilight, like the hush at
twilight, when everything living takes a breath and
listens to the sun set the west.

She'll make me feel like I've got something to say,
like my ideas are honey, thick and sweet and good.
She'll turn my ice to butter, and I'll spread smooth
again real quick.

And she'll love books. She'll read beautiful words
and let them sink deep into me. She'll open books
and let them whisper to me and slide me open.
She'll sail me away on words.

She'll collect my memories like Easter eggs and let
me hold them so warm and let me paint them so
sweet. I'll tell my stories to her.

If I write me a poem so sweet she'll say, "Your ideas are molasses.
I could just hear you all day long."

She'll let me write my words and my pen's going to
glide like bamboo through water. I'll sing my
words right out onto paper. She'll let me write so
sweet. She'll open button boxes of words,

bright ones, and high-class words so fancy to make
my writing shine, and fat black ones to hold
sentences from slipping, and smooth ones to use
real careful each day.

She'll let me choose,

let me say it like I feel it, let me hold time so still 'til
I'm done. I'll have words. They'll be attached to my
insides and sewn in.

When I wake up in the mornings I'll feel new like a
fresh March crocus up past the snow. When I go to
school, I'll sail like a water strider on a stream. It'll
be warm where she stands waiting.

One September I'll have me a teacher so sweet. I
Won't have to cry so long inside my heart or push
so hard to be seen because

I'm going to be somebody, sweet. I'm going to be
so sweet. 🙐

October 22:
Fourth Grade Classroom

Judy Michaels

The children enumerate houses,
igloo, teepee, longhouse, cabin,
skyscraper, shell, cocoon.
"Grave," she says.
She is ten
and leads them through the forest of wild hands
to a clearing.
They are thrilled. They are pure vibrato.
How did she think of that?
And I wonder, should we all go back
to "chrysalis," a pretty word,
and what happened to Charlotte when she wove
her sac of spider eggs?
"Grave," she says.
Discovery has so many colors.
Who in here has visited a grave?
I leave it alone, but think how long
a tuning fork will vibrate.
Some day, deep in her own woods,
she will think "house," she will think "grave,"
and go with mop and broom, boxes and tears
to her mother's
in search of a clearing. ❧

Front of the Bus

Maryfrances Wagner

On the bus trip, I sit so my students won't see
the thinning spot I can't cover with tint.
I know it glows like a burning bush
where the sun has fingered its way in.
From the back, laughter trumpets past
snippets of small talk weaving together
on a slow float forward. No one sits,
for the first time, where I can add
connections to this patchwork of teen talk.
Years ago, I sat on the bus behind Ms. Krumsiek,
taskmaster of looming demands.
No one sat near her as she stared past
these same empty trees, heard
the same lumber of bus wheels.
Behind her back, we imitated how she
nodded off during the Hardy book panel,
boasted about prize-winning roses,
pronounced spelling's two *ll*'s like a *w*.
Yet we were her proud flock,
perched over our pens, thirsty for white paper
when she cannoned vocabulary in steady fire,
ready to guess a character's epiphany.
Once, delivering a book, I found her
standing among her hundreds of roses,
sunlight haloing her luminous face
as she clipped me a fragrant handful,
tucked one in my thick, brown hair.
For the year I inherited her classroom,
I searched for her handouts, imprints
she left on the blackboard, but found her
only in my voice instructing students.
Without a protagonist to lead us,
we each take our seat at the front of the bus.
In the rearview mirror, a stranger stares
back, her face with its own story. &

Carrying Water

Daniel Ferri

This is a stage
There are lights;
Joe . . . stop flicking them
And a curtain;
Mike is climbing it
Props;
Aaron . . . put that down!

A stage, in a gym, at a junior high
Cameras loaded
Sister is squirming
Grampa's here
The show starts in twenty minutes

Can I say my lines to you?
This actor stands as tall as my eighth rib
Stands under my arm which is raised to say,
"Aaron put that down, now!"
"Sally, get over there!"
"Mike, tuck your shirt in."

Can I say my lines to you?
She's got on a blue skirt
Got her hair cut yesterday
And her parents still know her as a little girl.

She shakes her fingers
Breathes deep
Looks up
With eyes that are focused inside
Her skin is pale with concentration

I keep my arm
A silly shelter
In the air
Lest I break this spell

Don't tell me I cannot use the word "precious" here
Someone has raised her and loved her for years
And all those years she has been theirs
Tonight, a little bit of her will step away
Tonight, she tests waters

Her breath is deepening
Eyes focusing
Spine straightening
Hands relaxing
And her words spill free

I am carrying water in my hands tonight
From a stream to a river,
From a river to the sea
It is clear, it is common, and it is precious

Cup these hands with care
Move them slowly
Think clearly
Make no sudden moves

Their only value
Is their shape
How well they can carry
This cargo 🍃

Lines for Ms. Margaret (1922–99)

June Langford Berkley

Lost in the last row of old brown chairs,
adrift in a dim sea of desks and darkness,
my fingertips felt the hard, scarred space
that spread before me—
knowing the names of others
who dreamed, dozed, rallied, and pressed
with their knives and pens
into this same flat world of wood and silence.

I memorized each carved, lost line
with the hungry flesh of my hands
and watched through the open doorway

(for Mr. A, long lost in his own tangle
of infinitive phrases, was wont to have the breeze)

across the silent hallway, into the sound of your classroom,
where full light from the sun
of every window fell through the west windows
and flashed across the movement of your body
and the warm brown waves of your young widow's hair drawn back
like a nun's, I imagined, and slanted
across the page of the book
in your hand.

You turned those pages
as if your fingers found and
sifted, lifted sheets of gold;
the words from other worlds
flowed out of you,
rose up beneath us
out of some endless lake of language
shaped into bright eddies,
rushing rivers—
and settled into shimmering lakes
around us.

I want to remember how all the faces
leaned forward across the distance,
how, with wonder,
their hands, their fingers, all
soiled and dainty, pointed, clean and callused, stiff, and blunt and lean,
followed your voice across the page
of "Pippa's Passes."

We walked with you on the streets of Asolando.

Then in the din and clamor of the hallway after
I saw you—see you still—
standing by the doorway,
alone in the sunlight, eyes aglimmer,
fixed on both the near and far away,
on so much more than the afternoon.
I heard you read
and felt the hush of time,
the end of distance,
the open space that would become my life. ❧

Teaching Dreams

Cecil W. Morris

I
In my meanest dreams,
I am a fiery teacher
who drives knowledge like nails
into students
and who brooks no foolishness.
No student dares to talk
unless I demand an answer.
They sit at attention
in their perfect rows
and listen as I lecture.
I accept typed themes
offered by trembling hands.
I smile and nod
when they thank me
for my rigor.

II
In other dreams,
students refuse to sit down
and will not divulge their names
They mill about my room,
talking to each other
acting as if I do not exist,
as if my words mean no more
than the buzzing of a fly.
As often as not, they leave class
before I finish,
and I thank them
for hand-scrawled responses
to my assignments.

III
Some nights
students return to me
like salmon to their spawning bed
They shake my hand
and sit across from me
and tell me what they have done
what they will soon be doing.
I remember all their names
and just where each one sat
in my classroom.
Still, when they tell me
what they learned,
it's not what I remember teaching.

Telling My Sister How I Taught a Lesson on Child Abuse

J. F. Connolly

Details.
Two days ago we made posters
for the Massachusetts State Commission
for the Prevention of Cruelty to Children
and yesterday I gave a lesson
on how to write about it.
Details, I told them. Details.

We made lists, wrote poems,
talked at the bruise of it,
and I felt like an estranged
lover who makes jokes to say
it doesn't matter—it's really
not real. I told stories.
I lied. And what I left out
was the sound of our father's
drunk craze in your ear,
how a secret in our house
was more than love's aberration.
I tried to laugh. I kept
the students light, everything
just right: light, light,
nothing large and heavy
like his body collapsing on yours
in failure he could never
understand. And it was all
all right until I thought
of you locked away again,
one more December, the Christmas
rush rushing all over you until
the world's light snapped—
a crack and it was off,

the nightmare on,
love never right
and every touch as wrong as wrong.

The details got lost,
and I told the truth. I saw
the night snow falling outside
hospital windows, you staring
at its drift through holiday lights.
I told them how I saw you,
sister, baby sister, pretty
little sister, still in the arms
of a dead father, how you are watching
busy shoppers road-stepping into crowded stores
and the whole city marching to the abuse of time. &

Soliloquy
Deena L. Martin

You let me write
about rain seeping
through gray wood
quilts of graveled paper
and buckets of tar
balanced on long arms
you let me write
until I could feel
the standing on the rooftop

I wandered
with copper-stained toes
through the pages of my childhood
holding hands with desert dragons
I closed my eyes in sandstorms
drank juice from pomegranate seeds
and heard my soliloquy on raven wings
until children danced
on the branches of my trees
and I am the mountain
I said I was

Teacher, you let me. ❧

Miss Brower Joins the Marines

Manfred Bottaccini

We've hired you, rather than another,
said the tired old man behind the desk,
because you are smart and so very tall
that you'll control or at least intimidate
the big, glowering eighth-grade farm boys
who sit angrily in the last two rows.

She spent ten months in a drafty room
arguing with vanishing passion
that knowledge and books are more important
than killing edible woodland birds
with their dad's old gun, or even better
than controlling plow horses on the east forty.

Mostly she smiled false but dazzling smiles
while fending off amorous country lads,
their beefy dads, and the unchristian minister;
deciding then, that nothing else could be worse,
after a painful underpaid year, she quit teaching
and happily enlisted as a female marine.

Earth Day, 1999: Shootings at Columbine High

Judy Michaels

Writing again with these kids by the pond,
under circling hawks and the echoes of shots
that killed those other kids yesterday near
the Rockies. Daffodils are wild in this wind
that chills the water. Words are too tame,
we thrust our hands in up to the wrist. They redden
with cold, it's hard to hold the pencils, spring
was just beginning to come.

A Teaching Fantasy

Margaret Hatcher

I teach.
Ideas and words are my business.
I toss them into the air
      and watch them float
            softly
                  as autumn leaves
                  (though with much less color
                          and grace)

They float around your heads,
      drift in piles on your desk tops,
            glide along your sleeves
                  and whisper-dance
                        around your ears.

Someday
      one may catch your attention
            and inspire you with its color—
                  at least for a season.

Dear Mr. District Superintendent

Theresa Johnson

My husband is an artist,
so I need to find a job.
Our baby has begun to eat
rice cereal and bananas,
signaling independence
and rising costs.
While father and daughter play
with inks and paint and clay,
I want to teach
English, history, French,
coach tennis,
bring up the rear
at a cross-country turnout,
advise your drama club.

I student-taught at Franklin High,
lectured on the modern world,
was struck by the inquiring
minds of teenagers.
"Do you smoke dope, Miss Johnson?"
"Can I hand this in later?"
"What's that on your face?"
I mastered use of the ditto machine,
filmstrip, and overhead projectors,
wrote beautiful multiple-choice exams,
while my mentor took naps
in the faculty lounge.

I've enclosed my resume.
My husband helped me
cut and paste my life together
until it fit on one neat page.
We agreed that the summers
I spent picking pears,

the French dips and salads
I served at the HiWay Grille,
and the hundreds of diapers I've changed
should be omitted.

My husband would be glad
to silk-screen T-shirts
for your drill team
while the baby whines and drools in her playpen.
Thank you for your time.
I look forward to getting my foot
on the bottom rung
of your salary schedule.

I Don't Think So

Elizabeth Thomas

Our class rocked with musical chairs
and everyone wanted to lead.
The class would stand in a circle
boy, girl, boy, girl
and Miss Gary would point her pistol
and through teeth as sharp as the prickers near our swing set
she'd snarl, "You!"
Each time under my breath I'd whisper, "Me, me—I can do it."
Finally one day as the scratched 45 started to play my favorite song
I led the class single-file around the room.
We marched past handprint stars and lace-cut snowflakes
past black and red boots melting by the radiator
past Miss Gary
arms folded stiffly across her chest
as if to keep from spilling onto the floor,
just waiting for someone to trip or burp or have fun.
On my face was a smile the size of Jupiter
and my seven-year-old arms and legs were swinging
like a pendulum gone mad.
"The cat gets the mouse.
The cat gets the mouse.
Hi Ho the—"
The music stopped.
But hold on!
I love this song!
"—the dario. The farmer and the dell."
The room was quiet.
I looked around.
No friendly chair in sight.
Uh, oh—now I was in for it.

Even my best friend, Barbara
who shared Dixie cups with me from the same wooden spoon,
just scrunched her mouth

like my mother does when I spill the milk.
And I started to feel like that spilt milk
and wanted to puddle myself on the floor.
I wanted to do anything so I wouldn't have to look at Miss Gary.
When she scrunched her mouth
the whole school shook.
Classes down the hall would "duck and cover."
She was a real pain about rules.
Rules were made to be followed
and she was the teacher to show us the way!
And when one of us chose a different path
just the look in her eyes
would rip pictures off the walls
send chalk dust in all directions
make the toughest seven-year-olds pee their pants.
"Elizabeth, you did not follow the rules and—
WHAT MAKES YOU THINK YOU CAN SING! GIVE IT UP!"
The whole class cracked up—HA HA HA.
I wanted to bite off my tongue
and bury it during recess or
slip inside my pencil box
hide between the black and the blue.
Anything, but sit there and be laughed at.

We all have a story like this.
A dream we've tucked back into its box
because someone else told us—
we weren't good enough.

I did not sing again—for years. ❧

For English 200

Janet Warman

On pancake mornings
if my mother let
the griddle sit on the burner
just long enough,
when she would splay her hands
over its top, shake
water from them onto the surface,
the drops would dance,
spin and twirl
hissing up clouds of steam
until they disappeared to vapor.
Although she seemed to think so,
there was no correlation
between the jigging beads
and the success of her creations.
So often the first one turned
tree-trunk brown as she looked away
or mushed in the middle
with globs of ungelled batter.
I didn't care.
It was the dance that I would wake for.
Years later, trudging
up the stairs of Alamance,
Lit. books, class notes in hand,
before I even get to the door
some mornings I know:
Today! The drops will dance!

Ganado Trading Post

Suzanne Bratcher

I come to the Navajo Nation
to high desert and ponderosa forest,
to hogans and trailers and stucco government buildings
to trade my briefcase of lesson plans, handouts, and rubrics
for a smooth clay pot painted with black lightning,
a heavy silver bracelet and a string of turquoise fetishes,
a rug woven tight from root-dyed wool.

[Beauty before me . . .]*

I come to the round concrete school,
to computer labs and a satellite hookup,
to books about kids who ride subways, not horses
to barter my Kinneavy triangle and modes of writing
for mutton stew and frybread,
stories of yucca shampoo, sacred corn pollen, and squaw dresses,
ankle-length skirts and wine velvet blouses.

[Beauty behind me . . .]

I come to the spacious classroom
to a semicircle of kneehigh tables,
to teachers with soft guttural voices and worried BIA eyes
to offer my permission to nurture the children of the Diné
for piñon nuts and cedar and Mormon tea
dust devils that cross and recross washboarded roads,
sounds of goat bells and meadowlarks and thunder.

[Beauty below me . . .]

I come to the mesa,
to canyons, dry washes, and dusty red buttes
to ancient ruins of cliff houses huddled beneath an overhang
to hunt raven with black-fingered wings,
gather glazed blue rain that hangs in a pale tin sky,
collect vast silence and the courage of the bear,

[Beauty above me . . .]

to wander on the Trail of Beauty.

[Beauty all around me.] &

* "On the Trail of Beauty" is a blessing from the Navajo Nightway Ceremony.

Keys
Sally M. Oran

Jeff holds it up, then
Presses to my palm the small, silver thing and
At once I am seven again, feeling the rough buzz of concrete
Under the wheels of my skates.

He says, "My drum key,
Used to tune the skin. It tightens
As it turns and the skin is stretched to the proper pitch."
Could be. Looks like a skate key to me.

Then I see the twin natures of both tools.
Each with silver wings outstretched to which
Our fingertips can grasp and press to
Turn the key just so.

The pit at the tip of the key
Is just the shape of the bolt we choose, on skate or drum.
We each wield a twist of the wrist to secure our instrument
To sound its voice.

A turn and a turn and a turn—
And I am safe on tight-fitted skates and
Jeff rides free on the truly tuned
Hum of his drum.

October 12: Student Conference

Judy Michaels

Suddenly hot, red, wet as fever,
I lean over this young girl's poem—
my chemistry's gone haywire
and hers is just beginning
to make hay. "My mother," she chants,
"with the open heart door,
my mother and I." Her voice is proud,
she's put on words and knows
she looks great: "My mother and I
with our milk-flowing necks, my mother
and I with our emerald-chocolate-streak eyes."
She's learning who she is—cloth, color,
and cut. She can't believe
how much she knows. "My mother
with the nose of the fastest dog detective."
Words used to knot and tangle on the page,
but now she combs them smooth
or curls them and twists them to her liking.
"My mother and I . . ." The room's too small
for her and me and words and
mothers. We tear down the walls,
sun and grass give way before our dancing.
My mother leads the way, her dying cells
on fire. "My mother and I," Ali sings,
"with our laughs as sweet as brown sugar on apples."

Elbows

Daniel Ferri

"Give me an elbow"—
I give my students an elbow when things go right . . .
A good job gets one.
A better job gets a one, two.
An even better job gets a one, two, crossover, turn around . . . behind.

When I first taught school,
I would place my hand on a back whose owner just crossed some finish
Line only we could see.
More public victories
They got a big deal–big smile arm around the shoulder
Mugging for the camera.

I touch my students because humans need touch,
To say, "This is good," to hear it, and to know it.
But I don't touch backs any more.

When the principal calls a teacher and says
"I need to talk to you after school"—
The spine gets hot, the skin crawls
Just like it did when we were students, not teachers.

"What about?"
"I'll tell you then"—
Then
Two girls said you touched them—
"Where did he touch you?"
"On our backs . . . near the neck."
"Did he say anything?"
"He said, 'Don't do that'"—

"Now you tell me what happened"—
"It's like they said—
They were making fun of Margaret . . .

I thought if I made a big deal of it they would get mad and take it out on her."
"Well, they did, but they took it out on you—

"You don't have to worry.
It's over—
I spoke to them,
I spoke to their parents,
And I just wanted to talk to you.
Don't worry.
It's over."

No . . . it's not . . .
Smell,
I can still smell the stink of fear and shame on my skin.
What had I done to make them say what they said?
And what fit of fear or grace kept them from lying whole cloth?

If they had, you, everyone I know,
Everyone I meet,
Everyone who reads the paper
Would swear they could smell that stink still.
It would never wear off
No matter how many times I scrubbed my hands
In the sink of the 7-11 I would manage for my new career.

Give me an elbow.
A good job gets one.
A better job gets a one, two.
An even better gets a one, two, crossover, turn around . . . behind.

I touch my students
Because humans need touch
To say, "This is good," to hear it, and to know it.
This is part of our fabric.

But I touch my students with my elbows
Because I
Need armor. ❧

Learning to Read

Marty Williams

The teacher asked me
to recite the alphabet
before I left on a boat
for Anchorage, Alaska.
All those bored Boise Basin faces
at Central Elementary,
children struggling
with their A's, B's, and C's.

    Did she think
    we weren't ready
    for words?

They teemed in our heads
like lumbering ants
amassing weight
crumb by crumb
    elm
    linoleum
    porcelain doll
streamed
from our mouths
like dragonflies
when we played secretly
in the graveyard
near grandmother's house.
    Piper Cub
    Bing cherry
    grapevine
    everlasting

I was ready for more.
But I performed her small duty,
stood on the stool
in front of the class,
fingers twiddling the lint
in the pocket of my corduroy pants.
I named all the letters,
two by two,
      AB, CD, EF,

then stepped down and out,
ready to board the big ship
and move on.

Free Lunch

Sara Holbrook

Bent and staggered
the man, like an onion
could bring tears to the eyes,
shedding loose layers of gray stains,
trousers dragging a wake through the
dust storm at his feet,
his eyes fixed on another place.
Indigenous to this landscape,
pungent, swaying in the morning stillness.

"He can't help it, he's homeless."
Child to adult, native to foreigner,
she explains to me, the day traveler.
I've been schooled to take the long view past his kind.
Only eight years old, she takes the short view.

She knows I am out of place, in need of educating.
What kind of place I come from she doesn't know.
She sees me exiting my car every day and
she assumes my place is different.
She is right.

She is overflowing with last night's bedtime story.
How some guy tried to break in,
How her dad stuck a shotgun through the screen door, knocked out the bad
guy's teeth.
Later, six nine-year-olds
hold a cabinet meeting to decide if Dad should have blown the guy's head off,
would the blast have raised him off his feet,
how far the pieces would have scattered.

Thinking of my night,
last night, I remember there were clearly stars, unencumbered, just the hang
nail of a moon,
sounds of leaves mixing it up overhead.

I walked the dog.
Kids in my place, during storms they count the seconds
between the lightning and the thunder
to help keep the scared away.
Here, kids count the hours between the
gun shots and sirens and the scared never goes.

In my place, bathtubs are where you go to get clean.
Here, clean is what you want in a mom
and bathtubs are a place to get out of the crossfire.

She stamps my passport with a smile and helps me with my bag.
Together, we climb the steps into the trashcan
metal rattlings all around
foot-jammed full of yesterday's promises,
wrapped up in the same old news,
a gathering place for roaches and rats,
battleworn, sagging, and bruised.
For lack of another term, we call it school.
And funnier still, they call me teacher.

Kids in my place come to school with their backpacks stuffed
with lunches and supplies.
Here, the kids arrive empty-handed,
heavily laden with knowing
knowing how to conjugate cockroach,
knowing how to calculate time served.
Knowing about everything there is to know about how folks multiply and
    divide.

All these tomorrows being fed nothing but
leftovers.
Kids in this place will tell you straight up,
there ain't no such thing as a free lunch.

I stand in the classroom window
and see the man still stationed at the corner.
Today's lesson.
He can't help it, you know.
He's homeless. ❧

A Charm in His Arms

Jessica Barksdale Inclan

In fifth grade, I never did new math,
hiding behind a novel, excused
because my teacher seemed tired
of explaining how letters
could sometimes be numbers, exhausted
by my stares and laughter.
Finally, he had a heart attack,
and before math, the substitute, who must
have been warned, picked me up under
my arms and whirled and winged me
in a tight circle, the air pushed from
my lungs by shock, surprise, joy.
He sat down with me on pillows
and asked me to read during recess instead.

I made him pumpkin pies and cried when summer
came and I went on to sixth grade
and puberty, and harder
years, but his name comes
back to me now, Mr. Musante,
a name like a cello, an oboe, dark purple wine,
grapes, ripe melons, sun,
bites of deepest chocolate, a name
like the electric air around
my body as I swung like a charm in his arms. ❧

On My First Year of Teaching

Margaret Hatcher

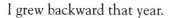

I grew backward that year.

Something like a whirlwind rushed me
        breathless
to the brink of an insane young world
        of screaming emotions
        and
        desperate, frightened eyes.

The torture of adolescence
        the blurred edges of fantasy
        stretched
        and
        pulled
        into my daily, tedious madness.

That year
        I rushed straight from complacency
        to collide with mirrored lunacy:
I had hoped to help
        (or for asylum, perhaps)
        but I found myself an alien
                a spy
        and as closed as a fist.

I wanted to tell them I was lost, too,
        but I saw only their deer-wide eyes
                shrugged shoulders
                shuffling walk.

An anachronism in sedate blue,
        I stepped quietly
        into my own fatigued days
                and bed-tousled nights

and put on my straightjacket too.

Bulletin Board

Ann Neelon

When I discovered that all the postcards of black authors
      had been defaced,
I heard my voice cracking, as in a radio transmission from outer space.
The world was waiting for me to deliver an important message,
      but I was an astronaut, not a poet.
The best I could do was paraphrase someone else's efforts:
"That's one small step back for a man, one giant leap backward
      for mankind."

Through the window of my classroom, I could see the
      Columbia Point Housing Project
      rising up in front of me like a lost planet.
Asphalt and cinder blocks were its most distinctive surface features.
I remembered the alien boy who had landed from there in my classroom.
When I called on him to read, he had inched his long black finger
      across the page,
      sounding out each syllable as if he were in second grade.
By the end of a week, he had given up on other universes.
I imagined him back in the projects, leaping up for a jump shot
      into a basketball hoop without a net.
He had been recruited as a basketball star. I heard the basketball
      bouncing, bouncing, bouncing.
"Don't blame us, we didn't do it," my students insisted.
      "Don't blame us, don't blame us."

I studied, below me, the small white dot of each worried face.
Earth, with its oceans and rivers, mountains and forests, kept
      swirling and swirling.
I said, "Léopold Sédar Senghor was the president of Senegal
      as well as a poet.
He was born in Joal, a fishing village where I once ate tortoise
      meat and rice out of a bowl with my hands.

At low tide, we'd wade out to a shell island, where the granaries,
      on stilts above the water,
      looked like old people with thick torsos and skinny legs.
At dawn, the fishermen, in flowing robes, set out to sea in their
      tiny pirogues . . ."
I started with Senghor because his face had suffered the biggest gash.
One by one, I held up the defaced cards,
      praying and praying
      over the face of the earth.

Thank You

John V. Pyle

thank you for burning that book
I was beginning to think no one
        had read it
it is a dirty book
it bothered me when I was a boy
and now that I'm a man it bothers
        me more than ever
it's about people who feel lost
and are trying to make some sense
        out of life
who are trying to learn how to love
and who are angry about having to
        die
and all that other dirty stuff

thank you for burning it
you've made my life a lot easier
now I know who to call next time
        I feel lost
and can't make sense of my life
and need to hear about love
and am angry about having to die

thank you for burning that dirty
        book
but thanks a lot more for assuming
        responsibility for the future
I was starting to wonder
starting to worry
that maybe we'd have to do it for
        ourselves ❧

April Inhalation

Judy Michaels

Today the girlgroup who hang in the nurse's office
to drink cold water from the machine and inhale
all a girl needs to know are leafing out
new tans, bare legs, new brains damp
and curly, a little surprised at how sharp they are.
"How come you always wear hats?"
one asks me, the framing giggles
transparent as air. Oh to just ask
anything, why do you have such long ears,
where did you get your skin, when
do you expect to die and when you rake new grass
and burn it, do you leave gold behind?
I breathe into these pierced ears, noses,
and maybe breasts, how chemo takes your hair
away. Their round eyes make me wonder
where does it go, all the hair
of the world? Icicles, and Spanish moss,
and the comet streaming back every thousand
years, and those clouds we call
mares' tails? The girls inhale my scent of truth,
not quite sense, a perfume they didn't
choose, unlike their leaf-green nails,
ten crowning glories that have stabbed out
cigarettes in the dark, have taken stock
of new hair in strange new
places and point their own way
through the dance of endless questions
that is the greening of willows
by cold spring ponds.

Backwards Day

Daniel Ferri

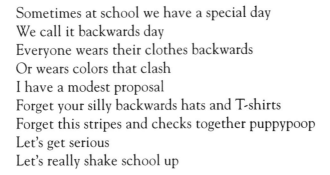

Sometimes at school we have a special day
We call it backwards day
Everyone wears their clothes backwards
Or wears colors that clash
I have a modest proposal
Forget your silly backwards hats and T-shirts
Forget this stripes and checks together puppypoop
Let's get serious
Let's really shake school up

In math class, for homework
Describe the associative, distributive, and commutative properties
In dance
Choreograph it, dance it, show your work
Points off for clumsiness

In social studies, for homework
Prepare two Civil War marching songs, one North one South
Sing in four-part harmony, show your emotion
Points off for flat notes

In English, for homework
Carve a sculpture that expresses Hester Prynne's solitary courage
The cowardice of her lover
The beauty and strangeness of her child

In science, for homework
Bring in a broken toaster, doorknob, or wind-up toy
Fix it
You get extra credit for using the leftover parts to make something new
Points off for reading the directions

On the S.A.T.
Every one of the questions
Will be in haiku

You get two scores
One in whistling, and one in Legos
No calculators

Let's take a stroll down the hall
Let's see who is in the learning disabilities classroom now
Will you look at all those guys with pocket protectors
Sweating, slouching, and acting out
Hey, no one cares that you can divide fractions backwards in your head
buddy
You will stay right here and practice interpretive dance steps till you
get it right

Will you look at all those perfect spellers with bad attitudes
Look at those grammar wizards with rhythm deficit disorder
What good is spelling gonna do you
If you can't carry a tune
Toss a lariat
Or juggle?

You are going to stay right here and do the things that you can't—
Over
And
Over,
And again,
And again
Until you get them right,
Or until you give up
Quit school
And get a job
As a spell checker
At the A & P 🐝

Marked for Life

Janie Reinart

Thin jagged line
Almost invisible,
(Because you can barely make it out)
Throbbing with pressure
Against the third-grade fingertip of your reading
W o o o o r d   b y   w o o o o r d
Like a scar
Marking the process of your struggle to learn
What the words are trying to say
Feeling the hurt
And uneven texture of the page
Blurred by tears
Knowing it will always show
Forever changing the fingerprint of your school life
Until someone takes your hand
And holds on oh so tight
Guiding your reading and thinking
Practicing strategies and praising you
Causing the scar to fade. ❧

No Picnic

Peggy Raines

It looks like a small picnic basket
brought to class this cold fall day.
But then, near the end of the hour,
it begins to shake and eventually cry.

Her stricken seventh-grade face pales,
begs my forgiveness, and confesses
she just couldn't miss the test,
she had to bring her . . .

So, dangling participles
give way to diapering,
and direct instruction
focuses on bottle position . . .

And I am reminded once again
that childhood is fragile
and fleeting
and all too often lost . . .

How I long to take her on a picnic
in the park
in the swirling leaves
before winter sets in . . .

From the Front of the Classroom

Elizabeth Thomas

From the front of the classroom
they look like apples
hanging from a tree
ready to be picked
faces smooth
skin crisp.
And I—
I feel old, overripe.
I have fallen from the tree
and lie rotting in the shade.
They could all be my children
including the teacher.

In a poster Scotch-taped to a colorless wall
Albert Einstein is also old (and dead)
but at least he looks distinguished.
Who am I trying to kid?
What can I possibly offer these students?
I am a poet.
I write.
I talk a lot.
When these kids come to school
technology is their teacher.
What knowledge do I have
that a computer does not?

When I went to school
we actually turned the pages
of outdated encyclopedias.
When we wrote letters
whole days existed before delivery.
When my mother wanted me in for dinner
she whistled through her teeth.
Now it's e-mail, beepers, cell phones

techno, metro, gizmo.
Even war is computer generated.
Death—a click away.
So, what can I offer these students?

Again, I look at Einstein
and this time read the words
"Imagination is more important than knowledge."
I am a poet.
This—I can offer them. ❧

Opposites

Eileen Snook

Overworked, overextended, overbooked.
Overweight, overtired, and overlooked.
      Overdrawn, and overhead,
      Overnight I'm sick abed.

Underdog, underpaid, undermined.
Underloved, <u>undermost</u> (that's underlined),
      Undervalued and underestimated.

      Undersigned,
        I. M. Underrated ⁊

Mr. Cohick's Physical Science Class

Maryfrances Wagner

Among thin-necked beakers, Mr. Cohick
perched over his lab table, waving long,
chalky fingers. We groaned at his puns
as he sent electrical charges sizzling
through wires or inspected our petri dishes
blooming germs we'd scraped from bathroom
sinks. To each of us he gave a nickname:
Charley Harley, Makish, Annie Mae.
One afternoon, while we drew cloud
formations, he told us how to figure
exactly when it would rain. As he dug
around under his lab table for his next
demonstration, I crossed my legs
to feel the texture of my silky stockings.
The memory of Eddie Arbor's breath
near my ear crowded my thoughts.
I rolled and unrolled my black turtleneck,
pinched my earlobe and watched shreds
of cirrus clouds inch over the stadium.
So then, what might this be, Cush,
his nickname for me. I fell through
layers of space. He held a long box.
Charley Harley stared. A thin whistle of air
rose from the heater, wavy as my thoughts.
Shrugging, I watched his eyebrows arch
like woolly worms. You don't know
what a thermometer is? Leady Eddie
humphed through his nose. Makish rolled
her eyes. I stared at thunderheads
sketched in my notes, felt them gather charge.
I sizzled Mr. Cohick, but I never forgot
how to figure when it would rain. ❧

To Walt Whitman

Margaret Hatcher

Walt, you shame me.
Desperately setting bones,
      bandaging and nursing the wounded,
      writing letters to the sweet boys' families back home
      by day,
writing your wild, passionate poems
      all night,
A nocturnal closet poet
      and a courageous and willing
      healer, warrior, visionary, and teacher
      with the sunlight full on your face.

I sit in the back row at faculty meetings,
      bored, frustrated, and secretly subversive,
      slumped in my seat
      scribbling invisible poems in code
while talk of budget cuts and legislative mandates
      leaves me closed as a snail.

I keep control,
      I withdraw,
      I do not break down, disappear,
      growl, or even whimper.
I simply move in my seat slightly
      while my spirit screams
      in the hollows of my bones:
            Save me! I am being held captive in a database!
            I am turning into a black statistic on a white printout,
                empty, predictable,
                and insignificant at the .5 level!
            Help! I am deeply wounded and
                need a gentle poet of a nurse!

Walt, you inspire me,
    a closet poet, too,
    to reclaim my own creative and focused spirit,
        to hold it like a candle in the darkness
        during the meanest and longest of hours,
    to honor my own
        healer, warrior, visionary, and teacher within,
    to find my voice, give my gifts
        without reservation and without hesitation,
        by the light of the moon
           or in glaring daylight.

The Long Answer

Jenny Nauss

Saturday night—
New faces from various places
mingle
The person to my right asks
>   the commonplace question
>   of the over-25 generation,
>   "What do you do?"

I am an actress
>   My critics tell me when I'm bad
>   and I don't mean as in good
I direct plays
>   Fate or free will? Star-crossed lovers meet their ends on our stage
>   I collect books and colored paper and old magazines filled with last
>   season's styles
>   The sign says, "Free! Take one!" and I take five
I am a gardener
>   A slinger of worms, a creator of compost
>   historian, social worker, environmentalist,
>   janitor, secretary, athlete, activist
Sometimes I embrace democracy
Sometimes I celebrate anarchy
Sometimes I reign in a monarchy where I rule as Queen

I seek answers in poetry, plays, short stories, and novels
>   from Conrad to Achebe
>   from Mishima to Radnóti
>   from Neruda to Allende to Szymborska
I have my own Top 100 list

I am a writer, a critic
>   My thumbs up or thumbs down determines futures
>   I must remember that

I love language
       The laughter it evokes when Pok
       new to our country
       greets the furnace man with a cry of
       "Wazzup dude!"
       The anger it releases when Vanessa
       reads her poem on the anniversary of
       her best friend's
       suicide
I keep Band-Aids in my desk and
       carry extra Kleenex to graduations and funerals—
I could go on but
because I suspect you want the short answer

I reply, "I am a public high-school teacher."

"Oh, that must be such a challenge."
And you walk off to get another beer. ❧

Undivided Attention

Taylor Mali

A grand piano wrapped in quilted pads by movers,
tied up with canvas straps—like classical music—
birthday gift to the insane—
is gently nudged without its legs
out an eighth-floor window on 62nd Street,

dangles in April air, Chopin-shiny black lacquer squares
and dirty white crisscross patterns hanging like the second-to-last
note of a concerto played on the edge of the seat,
the edge of tears, the edge of eight stories up going over, and
I'm trying to teach math in the building across the street.

Who can teach when there are such lessons to be learned?
all the greatest common factors are delivered by
long-necked cranes and flatbed trucks
or come through everything, even air.
Like snow.

Snow falls for the first time every year, and every year
they rush to the window
as if the snow were more interesting than math,
which it is.

Please.

Let me teach like a Steinway,
Spinning slowly in April air,
So almost-falling, so hinderingly
Dangling from the neck of the
movers' crane.
So on the edge of losing everything.

Let me teach like the first snow, falling.

Because my students asked me
what I would want them to do
at my funeral, I told them:

write and perform a collective poem
in which each of you says a line
about what I was like as a teacher
about how I made you reach for stars
until you became them
about how much you loved
to pretend
you hated me

you mean even after you die
you're going to make us do work?

On Wiesel's Night

Thomas E. Thornton

I cannot teach this book. Instead,
I drop copies on their desks,
like bombs on sleeping towns,
and let them read. So do I, again.
The stench rises from the page
and chokes my throat.
The ghosts of burning babies
haunt my eyes.
And that bouncing baton,
that pointer of Death,
stabs me in the heart
as it sends his mother
to the blackening sky.
Nothing is destroyed,
the laws of science say,
only changed.
The millions transformed into
precious smoke ride the wind
to fill our lungs and hearts
with their cries.
No, I cannot teach this book.

I simply want the words
to burn their comfortable souls
and leave them scarred for life. &

Teacher

Janet Warman

No mother taught me this:
to stand alone
before resistant children
and whirl the air
until I catch them in my web.
But when I leave the room,
all caught—myself
as well as they—
it is the mother
that I want to turn to,
to roll into her long skirts
and feel myself a thing
becoming. Slowly,
past oaks, past arches,
I let the magic trail me.
No mother knows that
in this place
the calling is asked
and answered every day.

New Class

Diane Aro Zobel

It's like a sleeping infant
in the first weeks you have her home.
You long for the perfect blend
of gentle, filtered sunlight.
You guard her tensely against jarring noise,
but you yourself,
inside so jangled
your edginess disturbs her rest.
She makes muffled, mysterious sounds;
she whimpers and shivers,
and you hold your breath,
wondering what kind of mother you will be
to this uneasy dreamer.
Then one day she awakens,
insists that the sheltered room be flooded
with vibrant colors,
and the exuberant sound of her voice
echoes and re-echoes off the walls.
The essential struggle begins
when she demands to tell you,
in words of her own creation,
who she really is. ❧

Teachers' Poetry about

STUDENTS

INTRODUCTION

Teachers' Poetry about Students
Peggy Raines

Teachers and learners are correlates, one of which
was never intended to be without the other.
—Jonathan Edwards

I n a restless night's dream, a student from more than two decades ago reappears and lives the life I always imagined for her. And recently, on a summer hike, upon passing a group of noisy teenagers, I am reminded of a field trip to a similar location during my first year of teaching, and am amazed that I can even recall the names of many from that very first ninth-grade English class of 1972: tall, handsome Joe, who devoured Vonnegut and Brautigan; popular, vivacious Yolanda, a natural leader whose clear articulate voice commanded attention; tiny, shy Jessica, whose poetry made us all weep.

The relationships between teachers and students, so powerful that they transcend time and distance, are really the reasons we return to our classrooms day after day, year after year. Even if we start our teaching careers wedded to a subject, we soon realize that it is the students who form the real content of teaching, and helping these young people make sense of their lives is truly the curriculum of consequence. Everything else is simply a vehicle we use to move us along the shared journey.

Certainly, it doesn't take teachers long to understand fully that the real joy and meaning of teaching come from the personal and intellectual growth of students, not simply the accomplishment of objectives or state standards. Watching the excitement in students' eyes as they finally figure out that wretched problem that has plagued them for weeks, hearing their heartfelt pride in explaining a new accomplishment, sharing their pain in a time of loss or grief— these moments bring each of us right to the core of why we teach. Connections of heart and mind renew us and reward us in ways that perhaps only teachers can truly recognize and appreciate.

Certainly, however, the profound impact that students have had on our lives as teachers is not always positive or pleasant. Who among us, when confronted with a particularly difficult student, has not struggled to find that "ethic of caring" we pride ourselves on, when, really, we would prefer to have a magic wand that would make him or her disappear from our classroom and lives forever? And, perhaps, in those particular moments, with those particular students, it is then that we become the students, and they, the teachers. For, surely, teaching is not just about the growth of our students, but also about our own development and growth as human beings. And out of those times comes new wisdom, often born in the shadows, not the light.

And, finally, who among us has not felt the immeasurable sadness of loss at the end of a semester, a year, or even, all too often, a young life? When we see dreams unrealized, potential unfulfilled, we torment ourselves for years with self-doubt and that often repeated question, "What else could I have done?" Who has not regretted those hurtful words we said in anger or frustration, or maybe worse yet, the words that went unsaid? And so it seems the endless worries about the well-being of our fragile fledglings continues far beyond reason or expectation, year after year.

So, in celebration of all of us who walk the path of teacher, may the poems that follow in this section bring us new insights, remind us of old heart connections, inspire us to continue, and reward us for all that we have done and been in the lives of countless students across the ages. ❧

CONTENTS OF THIS SECTION

CONTENTS OF THIS SECTION (continued)

Dark Nights

Ron Loewe

How grateful I am
      for that worn brown envelope
      tucked into its special place
      behind the books.
Often lately,
      I open its torn mouth
      and let it speak to me
      in past tenses.
I reach tenderly into its
      bulging cheeks
      and pluck bits and scraps of paper,
      notes,
      and letters,
      and listen.
How naive,
      these students
      to think that I would not horde
      their thoughts,
      feelings,
      hopes,
      and frustrations when
      they sign them . . .
            Love,
They jab into my heart,
      and mind,
      and gut.
I use them to patch holes
      in my dark nights.

Whooping It up at the MTV Saloon

Sara Holbrook

The gimmes, the grabbers
ripping the models out of the box with scissors,
stabbing at the protective cellophane with
sharpened pencils.
Scavengers who want to know rivers so they
plunge half a league onward into the valley
of sitcoms and talk shows looking for truth.
Tygers Tygers burning bright, pacing a
sprawling landfill of words so many before have
trodden black.
Those who do not go gently into any place we once thought good.
Instead, they whoop it up in the MTV saloon,
ignite canons in the faces of their teachers,
violently proclaiming that nothing is right with this world.
The blasted, jelly-boned swine, the slimy, belly-wriggling invertebrates,
the miserable sodding rotters, working to decompose
all our quaint and curious volumes of forgotten lore.
Vampires with jabberwock jaws that bite and claws that catch—
lords of flies,   apes of wrath,
shall I compare them to a summer's day—
          or simply death and taxes?

How do we love them?
Kids who want to line the cat box
with all the best laid plans of mice and men?
Who fervently believe that NOTHING depends on that stupid
little red wheelbarrow, and while they are entirely too wizened
to hazard any enterprise that might require new clothes,
          they are innocent enough to call themselves alternative.

Little lambs, who made thee?
As if we didn't know. They were conceived by the dashboard light
on the torn upholstery of the backseat of our discontent,
whereupon we loaded their toy boxes with a warehouse

of childish things, which they gave up as we booted them
into the wasteland.   Adolescence.
Now, they're back, headbanging against the door of adulthood.
Let me ask you, who the hell was it who said
when they come home, we HAVE to let them in?
(Frost)?   Do they know that? Don't count on it.
They think that the same guy wrote *Tarzan*, *Flubber*, and the story of
Moses presumably from his teepee on the shores of Gitchee Cumee,
that from here to eternity is the ultimate bungee jump,
and Uncle Tom is that guy who keeps sending them socks for Christmas.
        That literature went out with turntables, typewriters, and bosoms.

And now they want to write. Call themselves poets.
Didn't we invent TV so this wouldn't happen?
We put life on the shelf and gave the sexton the key.
We relegated passion to pay-per-view and appointed Hallmark love's
designated driver.   These kids weren't supposed to burn their
candles at both ends, we stocked up on long-life bulbs,
declaring that light lovely enough, thank you.
We named their dolls for them. We put their wars on computer screens.
Wouldn't you have thought that would have made them content to pad
around on little cat feet and stick to the study questions at the back of the
book instead of trying to write their own?   Based on what?
The world according to Jerry Springer? Bart Simpson? Erkle?

Do you think any one of us shall ever see one of their poems laid equally
spine to spine with the likes of Shakespeare?
What can we expect from those who have not read up on how to wear the
albatross? Might they in ignorance don its wings, bypass the stacks, use
the library roof for a launch pad, and say good-bye to all their friends on
shore? Maybe, if we are really lucky, they will send back word
to those of us marooned in the shadows of our own academic doubt
that those clouds aren't lined with silver at all,
but in hyacinth and gold, proving once—and again—
        all that glistens is not old. 🎐

(. . . *with apologies to the Bible, William Blake, Elizabeth Barrett Browning, Robert Browning, Robert Burns, Edgar Rice Burroughs, Lewis Carroll, Geoffrey Chaucer, Samuel Taylor Coleridge, Emily Dickinson, Walt Disney, T. S. Eliot, Robert Frost, William Golding, Thomas Gray, Ernest Hemingway, Langston Hughes, John Irving, Joyce Kilmer, D. H. Lawrence, Henry Wadsworth Longfellow, Meat Loaf, Edna St. Vincent Millay, John Milton, Dorothy Parker, Edgar Allen Poe, Carl Sandburg, Robert Service, William Shakespeare, John Steinbeck, Robert Lewis Stevenson, Bram Stoker, Harriet Beecher Stowe, Alfred Lord Tennyson, Dylan Thomas, Henry David Thoreau, and William Carlos Williams.*)

For My Student Who Said, "That's for Children"

Judy Michaels

"I was afraid to write nonsense,"
you said, "I was afraid someone
might laugh."
         Your hair falls straight
to your waist, you are one smooth
sweep of a potter's hands, tall vase
made to hold water so pure
it reflects nothing but sky,

which is nonsense, as poetry must be.
It mistakes dour for door, cries out
names of the dead and waits a beat
for answers, calls the soul
"seesaw," "poltroon," "dancing
bomb," and sees blind.

Poetry doesn't know any better.
You with your grave eyes and well-ordered
charity, you must forgive it,
try to forget what you know,
let your tongue turn
in on itself and babble about green
skies the color of blood, let your eyes
roll thunder, cigars, white silk,
socks.
         Water laughs only when it meets
an obstacle. I want to hear shining
laughter break out in your hair. ❦

6 East, Line 100

Donald D. St. Clair

I've come again to see you, David,
To remember where you sat in my class.
Craggy, farm faced, sandy hair, those deep eyes,
Midwestern respectful you were
And a quietly able student.

They said there was a scene
When they handed your folks the flag
Neatly folded, your life too soon wrapped up.
They said there were ugly words and refusal,
Anguish screaming at War's ways.

Years have gone by since.
I've grown old, changed careers,
Married, moved, done all the things
You had no chance to do:
Graduation in June in the gym
Home in a box in cold November.

When I come to Washington
I always come here first
As your teacher that I was
To take the roll.
I'll come again to see you, David,
To remember where you sat in my class.

To a Sleeping High-School Student, or Sweet Oblivion

Samantha Dunaway

You lie there
head on your notebook
oblivious
to the spiral digging into your cheek
and the little puddle of drool collecting
on the carefully detailed cover.
You are oblivious
to the disgusted look
on the face of the pretty blond girl
you've been obsessing over—
she finally noticed you.

You are oblivious
to the sign your best friend
has just taped to your back
specifying where you should be kicked,
oblivious to the fact
that he just smiled at the pretty blond girl
who has stolen your heart and doesn't care,
and that she smiled back.

You are oblivious
to the teacher
who hasn't woken you
because she is tired, too,
maybe too tired to care
or maybe she doesn't want to embarrass you
because you opened the door this morning
so she wouldn't spill her coffee
and she is grateful for small kindnesses.

And you are oblivious
to the fat girl in the back of the room
who quietly traces the clipped line
of the back of your hair
with her eyes, oblivious
to the longing to be read in her eyes,
and the spit wad in her hair.

Cal Norris

Gene Fehler

In high-school gym class,
Cal could sprint the first five yards
on his hands, flip to his feet
and still beat the rest of us
to the end zone. He hardly ever talked,
never went out for teams,
though all the coaches begged him.

Lisa, my ex-girl, still laughs
about the night we saw him at the movies.
The hero died in his sweetheart's arms.
The lights snapped on while Lisa and I
shuffled up the aisle past Cal standing alone,
staring at credits sprinkling down the screen.

He didn't even try to hide his tears. ❧

Question Unanswered

William Winston

I heard her eyes,
a little sad today, speaking
in gray, soundless circles,
imperceptible except for the tears in her throat
that nearly choked the words out of existence.
She was afraid to ask a question.

I knew the answer but was impatient to give it
so left it struggling, gasping, and her in acquiescence to its promise,
which confused her, though she said she was not confused,
and I accepted her obedience as though it were affection and not
suffering.

After all, she had only come to hold open her wound
to see if I could see it, too,
would see it with her and hold it next to
something in myself that seemed familiar, and
draw off some of the blood to ease the pain.

Like Lilly Like Wilson

Taylor Mali

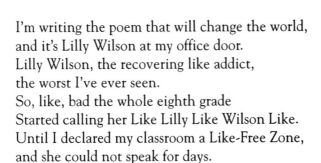

I'm writing the poem that will change the world,
and it's Lilly Wilson at my office door.
Lilly Wilson, the recovering like addict,
the worst I've ever seen.
So, like, bad the whole eighth grade
Started calling her Like Lilly Like Wilson Like.
Until I declared my classroom a Like-Free Zone,
and she could not speak for days.

But when she finally did, it was to say,
Mr. Mali, this is . . . so hard.
Now I have to think before I . . . say anything.

Imagine that, Lilly.
It's for your own good.
Even if you don't like . . .
it.

I'm writing the poem that will change the world,
and it's Lilly Wilson at my office door.
Lilly is writing a research paper for me
about how homosexuals shouldn't be allowed
to adopt children.
I'm writing the poem that will change the world,
and it's Like Lilly Like Wilson at my office door.

She's having trouble finding sources,
which is to say, ones that back her up.
They all argue in favor of what I thought I was against.

And it took four years of college,
three years of graduate school,
and every incidental teaching experience I have ever had
to let out only,

Well, that's a real interesting problem, Lilly.
But what do you propose to do about it?
That's what I want to know.

And the eighth-grade mind is a beautiful thing;
Like a newborn baby's face, you can often see it
change before your very eyes.

I can't believe I'm saying this, Mr. Mali,
but I think I'd like to switch sides.

And I want to tell her to do more than just believe it,
but to enjoy it!
That changing your mind is one of the best ways
of finding out whether or not you still have one.
Or even that minds are like parachutes,
that it doesn't matter what you pack them with so long as they open
at the right time.
O God, Lilly, I want to say
you make me feel like a teacher,
and who could ask to feel more than that?
I want to say all this but manage only,
Lilly, I am like so impressed with you!

So I finally taught somebody something,
namely, how to change her mind.
And learned in the process that if I ever change the world
it's going to be one eighth grader at a time. ❧

A Thank-You Note to My Student

Carol Reinsberg

Dear Amy,
I ate your rose last night.
It was delicious.
And this morning when I spoke to my
Senior English class,
My words were yellow
And wise
And filled the room with their sweet scent.
The students sniffed the air and wrote the words down
In yellow notebooks,
And they all got A's on the test.

One of them asked, when he saw his grade,
"Why haven't you taught us this way before?" ❧

Kids   —for Matthew Shepard

Kathi Baron

Kids wade through treacherous waters
every day, relish even, insistent
pull of current across newly
fringed calves and blossoming chests,
the thump of primitive rhythms
herding them through a furry
oblivion, ablaze with prickly sensation.
They trust the wily transient
in the park, the glittering
rocker pandering euphoria, easy escape,
parents who don't practice
what they preach.

Kids like Matthew Shepard
wade through treacherous waters every
day, relish, if they dare,
the hard pull of cross
currents in their aching souls,
harken curiously to primitive rhythms
beckoning them upstream to sunlight.
They trust teachers to honor diversity,
politicians to legislate safety,
parents to guard them from hate,
anyone to break the silence.

Kids like Matthew Shepard
trust kids who pound sense
into thin skulls, kids who
string them up, like scarecrows,
to warn kids like them
"Do Not Cross Here." 🐚

Editor's Note: Matthew Shepard was a gay college student who was kidnapped, robbed, beaten, and left to die tied to a fence in Laramie, Wyoming, in 1998.

With a Log Pencil

Susan Patton

With a log pencil I brand
tissue-like paper,

The doy sees the bog run.

The predator swoops down on me,
Mrs. Wing,
and I pray that she will fly away.
Scarlet ink droppings cover the sheet.
"You are not trying," she screeches,
"look closely at the sticks,
b to the left—*d* to the right."

---

boy boy boy doy boy doy

But the lines have a will of their own.
With blackened eraser, I remove the offenders
leaving black smudges to scar the page.
Once more I rub the paper shreds.

The light flickers off and then on again
and twenty-eight eager second graders
laughing—take flight to recess.
The vulture looms over me squawking,
"Sloppy seat work."
As she pecks at my work,

I slump over my desk in silence
to the sounds of hopscotch and creaking swings.
I am alone again to
battle with the uncooperative sticks.

---

b b d boy *d d d* bog

Which side is left? ⮁

84

For Ronald

Melissa Callaway

After your funeral, I went to school
and sat in your last row,
third seat, perfect attendance
desk.

Closed my eyes . . .

There you were in the hall with sagging, oversized
Levi's silver-tab jeans
    and a well-worn white T-shirt,
Your idea of a school uniform.
Rolling those big doe eyes with little-girl eyelashes at me
    like I'd asked you to do some song and dance when all I wanted
    was a meager reply.
I heard you laughing, flashing sidelong glances when I tried to call
    your bluff, knowing
    you'd aced my tests too easily.

On graduation day, I folded your cap and gown,
    removed it from the long stage chair you never sat in:
    violently taken from us so very young.

I went to school,
sat again in your seat,
found your cheat sheets, folded like love notes,
stuffed by your desk in the accordion wall. ❧

ℬrian

Sally M. Oran

Brian.
A small fifth grader.
I'll never forget him.

His skin—the sad sepia of a heavy memory.
His look—a shiver of light, a flinch
As if it might be wrong to smile.

He wrestled with the chore of speaking a child's script
In a setting where those about him shouted and roared
And made little sense of their world or his.

He responded eagerly to learning,
Yet could not contain the results.
He was simply surprised by the joy of knowing.

It was so easy to win him.
A soft sentence could turn his mood to hope
To hope to hope.

We had traveled one school year together, he and I.
Two learners measuring our words carefully
To craft low gates across cold borders . . .

Privilege, hurt, fear, helplessness.
I, the disabled one.
Knowing nothing to do for him but teach.

He, the stronger, selecting lessons cautiously,
The ones that seemed to help
To open hope, to heal.

He was the last to go that May day.
I had spoken a personal word to each child.
Brian was the last.

I could not utter one word I wanted.
Only . . . "Be good."
And that through tears.

He and I both knew he was already good
In a world that was terribly wrong.
I should have shouted those same words to the world—

"Be good! Be good to him!"
Brian.
I'll never forget him. 🍃

Mi Palomita

Jessica Barksdale Inclan

I cannot describe you but to say
smooth hair like wind-whisked summer hills;
eyes deep and full of still, sorrowful water, brown
like the doves of your name.

Back home, years before,
your brother killed himself, jumping from the
red tile roof to the patio, his blood
a cool slick pool when you found him.
Before that, *banditos* kidnapped your father,
burying him underground for fifty days and nights,
waiting for ransom.
Later, here in this country, your fiancé backed away from
his promise, encouraged you
to go home to Mexico and let him be,
let him live without your manic crashes,
personality waves against small apartment walls.

Our first semester, you had a nose job, your
Aztec arch whittled to American bob, your
brown *caramba* hair tinted to suburban blonde,
your ass trimmed clean of tortillas and beans.

The next class, you were sleepy, drugged into tardies
and late homework, your eyes slack with charcoal rings;
the next day, you would whip around me like salsa notes,
handing me your favorite CD, urging me
to listen, to play it loud, to dance in the hallways
singing, *bésame mucho*.

Finally, when your sentences were more English than Spanish,
you told me truths about it all, the drug
combinations, the suicide slits
on your wrists, the days you couldn't stand the light, couldn't
stand to be alive.

Too late, months, maybe a year, later, I thought
to call, a strange man listing a strange family name on the tape,
urging me to leave my number,
I hung up, staring at the old roster, remembering how I told you of my own
sadness,
the days when I was afraid to open my eyes, knowing
it was impossible to go to the grocery store,
put lettuce in a plastic bag,
pay the clerk with a check.
I gave you books, called your doctor, talked
to your college counselor,
but I let the summer slip into fall and then winter without
knowing where you were, let all that
happened after your fiancé left you be unknown to me,
moved into my now happy life without a backward glance.

At least there still is this: a framed picture
you brought me from Mexico, plywood carved and painted
into overflowing maroon wine jugs, ripening bowls of red, seedy fruit,
Calla lilies wide open and beautiful,
tilting just slightly to the left. &

Bygone Dreams

Peggy Raines

It's been almost twenty-five years,
yet, my early morning dreams today
were filled with her,
now grown, beautiful, fit, vibrant . . .

How can a memory of one student
out of so many
stay so vivid
for all that time?

How can a bond
that strong remain today,
when I have no idea
where she is, who she is . . .

She wasn't all that exceptional
in the English classroom,
but, oh, on the basketball court,
she was remarkable . . .

She could almost outrun her
abusive alcoholic father
when she raced to the basket,
almost forget what waited at home . . .

More talented than any other
athlete I ever coached, cajoled,
encouraged, loved,
teary eyed with pride year after year.

I did hear, years ago, that
she finished college, but returned home
to relive the family pattern;
she married a man just like Daddy . . .

I can't seem to remember her dreams,
and I'll never know if they were fulfilled,
but my dreams for her
played out perfectly at 4:00 a.m. this morning.

With Apologies

Charles Atkinson

[Perpetual] is a silver bar turning end over end
. . . in freezing, starless space . . .
There is always more.

                    —from my student, Leanne

With such gifts so early, it will amaze you
yet to wake on a morning limpid as this and
combing your gloss to arm's length, find that
more is not shells on the beach, fluted for you,
or the slow rain of ingots from an affable god.

When *more* is taut silence between you
and a love, or the wrong words for what
you know, you may not bend to gather it gladly.
The white wave curling to the beach will
quit its soothing *toom, toom;* tradewinds
will die in the palms, even the palms vanish.

You'll be standing in a room poorly lit
when the envelope's sliced and the letter
falls open, when the call first comes, when
the few unspeakable words are uttered.

You, with eyes clear enough to welcome
the long light of arctic midsummer—
can I doubt you'll bind up your hair and
enter the leafstorm in your own lucid way?

This is from one who's seen the same bar
tumble in space and felt its celestial wind,
who knows there's always more and would
praise the less that's come of it—one who's
touched by your trust, and groping for a way
forward or back. Forgive me for throwing
sand in the wind; the wind will carry it off. ❧

Dance

Laura Benson

Attaching meaning to
Black ink symbols
On a page . . .

I looked at the words.
I knew they were words—
and I knew that everyone
got it
        but me.
I could not stay
with the words.

I became the best girl.
Cleaning erasers
Listening with eyes
on her. Always on her.
Sure that if I watched
closely enough
I would know.
But I never did.

I wore patent leather shoes
with white lace socks
so that she wouldn't
see what I didn't know.

The other kids
turned in a million
book reports.
How could they read
all those books
all by themselves?

I was sure
that I was really
slow.

The kind of slow
they speak of only
in whispers.
Did they forget
to tell me?

I just kept up
my good-girl dance
hoping they wouldn't
find out my secret
and send me away.

Stay quiet.
Be good.
Look good.
Maybe they won't know.

And one day,
the words became
pictures
     in my head
and feelings
     in my heart.
I heard Trixie Belden
and Charlotte.
I knew Charlie and longed
for a golden ticket
wrapped into
a chocolate bar.
I couldn't believe
all those grandparents
fit into that one bed!

With a book pressed against my chest,
I walked into class
knowing I was still slow.
But having *Follow My Leader*
and *The Little House on the Prairie*
and *Happiness Is a Warm Puppy*
with me,
I was a little faster now.
A little faster. 🙠

Final Impressions

Maryfrances Wagner

Every morning, I drive past the bent railing
under the willow, the spray paint still vivid,
though the crosses and wreaths are long gone.
Once my students tied laminated poems
on these branches, in memory of Kathy,
one of four students I've lost this way.
The neighbors left them up all winter,
Fluttering on yarn bows, some mornings
winking like Morse code.

I remember so well the day before,
Kathy reading her poem about Jeff,
her yellow bow bobbing as she shifted
from foot to foot. She sketched for us
the blue dress she'd sewn for prom
and dotted in her grandmother's pearls.

Usually the quiet girl hunched at her desk,
she pulled layers of hair across her face
and bowed her head when I asked for readers.
She pressed so hard when she wrote,
I could feel the puffy Braille of her paper,
read impressions left on the under page.

Afterwards, we read elegies, our eyes
drifting to jags of light reflected from her
empty chair. We walked to the funeral
as a class, our drawn faces watching
the shoes in front of us. We stared
at her picture framed on the coffin.
She wore the blue dress, the pearls.

Perhaps it is better to go in a heat,
after the slow dance beneath the spinning,
mirrored ball, breath warm on a bare shoulder,
moist hands clenched, a rose corsage wafting
its notes; knowing at last the sweetest juices.
The penultimate moment when we press so hard
before the oncoming car spins across the lane. &

Teacher Review

James Hobbs

And so, what did I teach you?
What do you remember from the dull hours,
in dull desks, reading dull books
and taking dull tests?
How did I rate you?

About three years ago, a woman
I did not know stopped me outside
my classroom door. She said,
"You don't remember me.
I was your student in the early 1970s.
No one knew me.
I was a cipher on the chart.
But you were kind to me and played
music from Jethro Tull's *Aqualung*
and *Jesus Christ Superstar.*
I have never forgotten that, and little
by little I began to like myself.
My life hasn't been easy, but
that music and your treating me like
I could understand it made a difference,
at least for me."

What could I say?
I thanked her for the kind words.
As she walked away, I called out to her:
"This is why I am a teacher,
for students like you." 🙐

Andre Morgan's Fresh Rap

Marty Williams

The obstinate Andre Morgan
rapping truths from his own world

tough as he can make them
cocky and transparent

hits a sound, or slip
slides around it

forcing rhyme to heel
to a fresh man's beat

he brags and struts,
fingers pop, joints lock

he calls it as he knows it
or, by another name,

the way it is, "the way
it's s'pozed to be,"

moving with his rhythm.
Making meaning with his rhyme.

Forced Entry: To My Students, with Love

Margaret Hatcher

With my foot in the door of your head
With a drop of light
With this bouquet of flowers
With shameless arrogance
        and laughter
With an edge of urgency
With the taste of salt-lipped beauty
With   silence
With clipped wings
With a vibration, throbbing in heartbeats
With gentle grace and prayer candles lit through the night
With my attaché case full of forgotten dreams and names
With a cutting edge
With the speed and agility of a runner who leaves no tracks,

I try to force into your head and heart
            these ideas
            these words

For Father Cardenal

Elizabeth Thomas

She's a foot tapping
pen clicking
hair flipping
eyebrow raising
head rocking
teeth sucking
"Who the fuck are you?"
kind of 90s
kind of girl

and she can't help but giggle
at the man who reads poetry
in front of the room
because, "Poetry is stupid."
He is unfazed
so intent on his words
and the history they convey.
In broken English and in fierce Spanish
he wants them to understand
the conviction of liberation
and how in a true revolution
nine-year-olds may lead armies,
die for a righteous cause.
Mockingly she turns toward her neighbor
rolls her eyes and fakes a yawn.
From both sides she is shushed.
"Why should I listen to him?"

Rocking in her chair
she mouths the words to a song
hands never still, tapping the backbeat.
Like a point of light in the dark
my own eyes track her,
and I blink at the flame.
She just can't sit still

so finally the teacher with Mrs. Potato Head lips
leans back and glares in her direction.
Like the poet himself
she is unfazed.

He recites a poem about
the beating of wings against the bars of cages
and how when he finally returned
to the mountains of his native Nicaragua
so many young people were dead or disappeared.
During this revolution
it was a crime to be young
he tells the audience of high-school students.
When he came home he kissed the ground
knowing it was sacred,
"a great tomb of martyrs."
"How can anyone just sit here and listen to this guy?
What is he talking about?
Except for his black beret
he looks like Santa Claus.
Where's my present?"

In a choked voice
the last poem is about a poet, his nephew
who shouts, "Free homeland or death"
and accomplishes both by the age of 20.
The word "death" has caught her roving attention.
"There ain't nothin' I would give my life for!
Get this guy out of here!"

He's a worn down
sandal wearing
gotta say it
Can you hear me?
inside out
out of time
kind of 90s
kind of poet.

"You can't teach me nothing!
Go ahead—I dare you!" ❧

Band-Aids and Five-Dollar Bills

Sharon Draper

My students wrote essays for homework this week,
The usual stuff for grade ten,
I asked them to write how they'd change the world
If the changing was left up to them.

His name was Rick Johnson; he was surly and shy,
A student who's always ignored.
He'd slouch in his seat with a Malcolm X cap,
Half-sleep, making sure he looked bored.

His essay was late—just before I went home,
It was wrinkled and scribbled and thin,
I thought to reject it . . . (Why do teachers do that?)
But I thanked him for turning it in.

"You can't cure the world," his essay began,
"Of the millions of evils and ills,
But to clean up my world so I could survive,
I'd cut Band-Aids and five-dollar bills.

Now Band-Aids are beige—says right on the box
'Skin tone' is the color inside.
Whose skin tone? Not mine! Been lookin' for years
For someone with that color hide.

'cause Band-Aids show up, looking pasty and pale,
It's hard to pretend they're not there,
When the old man has beat me and I gotta get stitches,
Them Band-Aids don't cover or care.

And now, you may ask, why would anyone want
To get rid of five-dollar bills?
'cause for just that much cash, a dude's mama can buy
A crack rock, or whiskey, or pills.

She smokes it or drinks it, and screams at her kids,
Then passes out cold on the floor,
By morn she remembers no pain, just the void,
And her kids wish the world had a door.

So my magical dream is not out of reach,
Like curing cancer or AIDS, or huge ills,
All I ask from my life is a little respect,
And no Band-Aids or five-dollar bills." 🙠

Something We Can Hold

Jessica Barksdale Inclan

Her name is Elizabeth, and she sits
in the back row,
hiding her bad teeth.
She bends her head, shallow
waiting tears
glinting behind her glasses.
Her hair is uncombed,
and she blushes each time
I call on her.
I cannot know her whole life, but my own
bursts with every
possibility as I read her papers,
clumped words
typed at a slant on a portable typewriter.
I read about her mom, full
of cigarette smoke and
spite, a woman who kicks her children
from her home like fledglings, but these birds
cannot fly, twisted teeth and ignorance all they carry.
I read her journal, trace
the messy circles of her words, breathing
in the ripe despair of her evenings.
I try not to imagine her future,
something full of blue-light
specials and aluminum siding, Elizabeth
in front of a computer in an insurance office,
stubbing out her cigarette,
cursing her children's grades and bad skin.
And when I stop imagining and look
into her face, I see a map for all of us,
my nineteenth year, full of a live-in boyfriend,
part-time jobs, and how I finally got out of there,
leaving retail and Robert for college and the rest of my life.
I see there are so many options,

everything leading to this one place
that is either right or wrong
or completely in-between.
I see that we can lurch by, moving past
that invisible moment
we can either cradle or crack in our palms.
We may never get to a place
where we can watch the curve
of our lives twisting
into something we can hold. &

Students

Karyl Goldsmith

insomnia
i lie awake staring through wide itchy eyes
It's cold and dark
the coyotes howl
i blame the strong coffee after dinner, but
i replay the day or the hours, sometimes seconds
did you understand the poem?
why were you so tired?
were you crying?
how can you live in a tent?
is that bruise really from soccer?
It's still dark
It's still cold
Dan is warm, but
even he can't help
the clock stares at me unblinking, too
the coyotes are grumbling—hungry
they sound like teenagers in class
i grin to myself, to my pillow
my day rewinds, play it again on fast forward

insomnia
i lie awake, dry eyes drooping
was your father drunk?
do you want to go to Harvard?
can you talk to your mother?
are you scared?
is that why you growled "bitch" at me?
It's not really my responsibility after all
the wind is bitter cold
the moon is gone
i stare at the blank sky
the coyotes are real
and i can't sleep

Cherokee Father/Son

Sally M. Oran

Sleek dark
hair like sure
Arrows secure in twin
Quivers down their backs
They are two hunters
Reading the space
Between them
As they
Walk.

Their pace
Predestined by
Genes, unison steps
Track their new history
Born centuries ago in the
Cradle chants of ancient clans—
Their paths now echo
That enduring
Legacy.

They stride
To the cadence of
Their separate identities
In perfect counterpoint:
One medicine song
Composed in the
Steady rhythm
Of two
Hearts. ❧

The The Impotence of Proofreading

Taylor Mali

—for the boys of
the Drowning School,
52 East 662nd Street,
New York, New York

Has this ever happened to you?
You work very horde on a paper for English clash
and then get a very glow raid (like a D or even a D-)
and all because you are the word's liverwurst spoiler.

This is a problem that affects manly, manly students.
I myself was such a bed spiller once upon a term
that my English teacher in my sophomoric year,
Mrs. Myth, said I would never get into a good colleague.
And that's all I wanted, just to get into a good colleague.
You know, not just anal community colleague—
because I wouldn't be happy at anal community colleague—
but one that would offer me intellectual simulation,
like an ivory legal colleague.
I know this sounds stereophonic, but I really need to be challenged,
challenged dentally.
So I needed to improvement
or gone would be my dream of going to Harvard, Jail, or Prison
(in Prison, New Jersey).

So I got myself a spell chukker and figured I was on Sleazy Street.

But a spell chukker can't catch catch every single missed ache.
For instant, if you accidentally leave word out,
Your spell chukker won't put it in you.
And God for billing purposes only
you should have serious problems with Tori spelling
your spell Chekhov might replace a word
with one you had absolutely no detention of using.
Because what do you want it to douche?
It only does what you tell it to douche.
You're the one with the mouth going clit, clit, clit.
Goes to show you how embargo one careless clit of the mouth can be.

Which reminds me of this one time during my Junior Mint.
The teacher read my entire paper on A Sale of Two Titties
Out loud to all of my assmates.
She made me feel like the dumbest stud in the word.
It was the most humidifying experience of my life,
Being laughed at pubically.
So do yourself a flavor and follow these two Pisces of advice:
One: There is no prostitute for careful editing.
And three: When it comes to proofreading, the red penis your friend.

Flow what I say, and I compromise you
You'll make your English torturer very, very hippie. _🙦_

Body Language

Jean W. Hicks

Slinking into his chair,
his rear barely graced the front edge of the seat.
Legs straight out
balancing on his heels
his head scarcely crested
behind the table in the corner where
he sat.

We knew his name
but called him Tolbutt
and laughed at the sound of it.
I can still hear the sing-song way
it was flung at him—
Tolbutt, Tolbutt.

Like farmer in the dell
and duck, duck, goose,
it was a game.
We circled
and he was out again.

Tolbutt
picks his no-ose.
Tolbutt
wets his pants.
Heeeeeee
eats his boo-gers.

Tol-butt, Tol-butt.
Out loud.
At recess.
In the halls.
At lunch.

And in class.

Not one teacher stopped us.
Not one head snapped up.
Not one, "What did I hear you say?"
Not one, "How dare you!!"
No "talking to"
No calling down the name-callers.
They ignored us
so we ignored him
for five long years.

Pretending not to care,
he continued to slouch,
looking unstarched.
He perfected a fluid walk,
melted into the crowd,
his neck flat
and his head poking out of his chest
like a turtle's
trying
to disappear.

Then there was the day
he jumped out of the shadows.
One taunt too many,
muscles taut,
eyes flashing,
he threw a fit
kickingscreamingrailing
bitingcryingpounding.

We were afraid,
for a minute.
Who was this crazy person?

He never did it again.
But he never sat up, either.

He just never sat up. 🙚

Autopsy Girl

Rick Stansberger

Ice-picked skulls
in X-ray light:
forensic medicine text,

the weirdest exhibit
I have ever received
when checking for plagiarism.

I had begun cautiously:
Kathy,
these details
in your murder story
are remarkable.
Where did they come from?

And she,
already immersed in a world
of accusation and defense,
calmly plops on my desk this tome.

"I like autopsies," she says.
"My uncle's a coroner.
I'm going to be a homicide cop."

I pick up
her twenty-page story again:
Um, these guns,
do you know how to use them?

She smiles.
"The .38 Smith
and the nine-mill Browning.
I've handled a Glock
but wouldn't trust
my life to it in the dark."

I mumble the usual
this-is-nice-keep-writing,
and she bounces off to physics
It is such a
normal-looking bounce. 🙦

The Cowboy in English   —for Rob Compton

Cecil W. Morris

I watch him not reading,
shifting in his seat,
uneasy as the horse in the chute,
and I wonder what I have to offer him.
He takes off his cowboy hat,
picks lint from its heavy black felt,
and then settles it on his matted hair.
He leans back in his seat, whip-thin
but tough, too, tough enough
that no one laughs at his tooled belt
or his wide rodeo buckle.

I watch his heavy-knuckled hand
slide his book across his desk,
watch him press his few words into his paper,
watch him watch the thin strip of sky
visible through the room's narrow windows,
and I know all that matters to him is outside—
the sharp bite of the January air,
the smell of dust and saddle leather,
the heat that rises from his horse
after he makes it lope around
and around his father's field.

I want to give him something he can use
when he no longer wants to take the fall,
when he's broken his last thin bone,
when his body finally betrays him,
or worse, when his spirit fails.
I want to give him something easier
than hard landings on hoof-packed dirt,
than lessons taught by the huge
sweating bulls of his experience. ❧

Sara Smiled

Sylvia Saenz

Sara smiled at me on Thursday
with a promise to share her poems
on Saturday night.

Instead, she packed her things on Friday
and headed west, across the desert
toward San Francisco and a man
who told her not to come.

On Sunday at Gila Bend
she was cited
for running a stop sign.

Monday found her purchasing courage
in Naco; tequila and tranquilizers
took her to the canyon . . .
where she would be found
on Tuesday, hanging from a tree.

Where's the poetry in that?

For a Student, on Leaving Seventh Grade

Timothy Hillmer

Leave the 1,260 pages of printed reading materials,
Leave the 154 miles spent walking to school,
Leave the 163 school lunches,
Leave the 12 spiral notebooks,
Leave the 42 pencils,
Leave the 38 pens,
Leave the 1,049 times you signed your name,
          double-looped as Daddy might want it.
Leave the 21 times you wished Dad dead.
Leave the 14 times you wished Mom saved,
          telling her so as you stared into mad eyes,
          her daily Valium, her evening bourbon,
          all her sweet notes sung to baby
          raked clean by Dad's dark fist
          cracking her jaw like a walnut.
Leave the red bandanna you wore in February,
          a wreath of roses blazing on your brow
          before being torn away amidst jeers
          of freak and hippie shouted by peers.
Leave the locker you shared with no one,
          the chalk drawings of mountains taped inside,
          Each set in a pastel sky.
Leave the pages of stories and poems
          you slipped on my desk
          each in the calligraphy of a spy.
Leave all you've learned about hate
          here in this room.

Take all you've learned about love,
where you sleep,
where you dream,
where you bloom. ❧

Absolution by Teacher

—for Laniel

Kathi Baron

You claim you've seen a Skinwalker
Shape shift into red coyote dust cloud,
Blind your grandmother among her sheep

Of course you were alone
When the doorknob turned, when evil
Scooted down the hall
Streaked darkly past your window

But I think shame cramped your wheel
That day, ruptured your safety
Like lamb's blood spoiling ceremonial clothes
Another girl's sacrificed innocence.

Not sin, but guilt tossed you like dice
'til you landed on shattered cat's legs
Broken but born to this life

Now you get another chance to forgive
A father who mistook you for his demons
Forgive yourself for tracking Christ's feral eyes
And finding yourself.

Cycles
Shirley R. Chafin

Why can't I remember your name?

You were the brunette trying to look blond
in the fourth seat of the first row
in my first-period English in '74 or '75,
or was it '76?

Your eyes did most of the talking
like guards in black uniforms sorting
through family artifacts, scoffing
at anyone who came too close.
Your themes were case studies
of a girl changing roles to please her parents,
surviving divorce, and being left
with an aunt to mature
like a seed dropped accidentally
through a hole in her father's pocket.

Some eight years later
We've come to the laundromat.
Your face serious and taut,
you lift from two heavy-duty grocery bags
a miner's coal-blackened trousers,
sort a two-year-old's cotton dresses,
and your own sweatshirts and jeans,
load them into separate washers,
deposit your quarters and wait
for the cycles to end.

Jonathan, Asleep in Class

Hillary Lyon

another late blackjack shift
cards sliding off the top   two up one down
casino light smeared festively
on the glossy retired faces
from Indiana Ohio Michigan New Jersey
another midnight shift smiling
under acrylic chandeliers

in class your once-starched shirt is a cloud
of cigarette smoke   your uniform-issue bolo tie
cannot lasso the lecture
lulling you   your teacher's hands
are silent birds with polished beaks
the assignments are pillows
stacked beneath your head

close your eyes   Jonathan
and your classroom is an air-conditioned womb
where dreams are
neither encoded in impossible
numerical combinations
nor clangorously dispersed from the chrome mouths
of slot machines

The Boy

Kathleen Lynch

alone in the yard
crosses the lawn halfway
and begins dancing,
his shadow a lively
dark spider monkey.
A little riffle of applause
runs across the birches.
The sun holds to its gentle
phase. Earlier, he practiced
dying, a soldier flung full face
down, then one who crumpled
slowly, then Stagger Man,
bent, clutched, slow-zigging
the whole green distance
as if he couldn't decide
whether he was more attracted
to grass or air. But now
he is dancing—a yanking,
loopy kid. What music
he hears, I can't. Was I ever
such a creature outside
of time? Now his arms
become wings. He runs full bore
the length of green, then in one
quick, horsey surge bolts
up, leaves ground. This
is where I'll leave him,
all virtuosity,
caught and held
by nothing.

Valerie
Lee Ann Spillane

How can I think
about homework
tests
tardies
research projects or
term papers?

How can I think
about time on task
sitting in your seat
hall passes or
after-school detention?

How can I think
about planning
units on freedom
or the faithful
when all I see is you?

Long mink-colored hair
swept behind your shoulders,
you sit with your brown
eyes swimming
in the salt of tomorrow's tears,
as you tell me

you are pregnant

and fifteen.

ℛevelation

Elizabeth Thomas

His T-shirt says, "I am God."
I think, "Well, my lucky day!"
I'll run up, shake his hand, ask for an autograph—
I might never have this chance again.
But, as God sits there
waiting to step into the Vice Principal's office,
I look closely at his faded T-shirt
two sizes too big
sneakers older than he is
thin legs swinging
barely long enough to reach the floor
dirty hands massaging a dirty forehead and think—
this is not God.
This is a little boy
who maybe swore in the lavatory
or tussled on the playground.
A child who probably forgot to eat breakfast
did not expect a good-bye kiss.
When he gets home from school today
he'll let himself in with the key
that hangs around his neck.
He might help himself to Twinkies and a glass of Coke
a microwaved pizza in front of the TV.

He struggles to raise his head
and the circles under his eyes slope toward his chin,
pick up the lines around his mouth
and carry them down as well.
It's not easy taking care of the world.

Using the back of his hand
he trails snot and tears across his face
into his hair,
which heads out in all directions

as if just lifted from a pillow.
He looks neglected
like homework over a long weekend.
This boy ain't been loved in a long time.
I want to walk over
kneel on both knees
use my sleeve to clean his cheeks
kiss his feet
tie his sneakers.
He looks up
and in his eyes I see my own son.
Unable to look away,
I want to say something
make some excuse
beg for forgiveness.
But—
this is God.
What could I possibly say
that he does not already know?

Weekend

Renee Ruderman

She went away for weekends
at fourteen, without a suitcase,
by herself, seeking a lover,

consumed by what she despised
in the mirror, a solitary, sad,
long-nosed girl, unsafe without

her secrets. In her room,
the floorboards gave strength;
she was away

behind the brass plate of her
locked door, writing, lying on her
stomach, building her world

of smooth architecture, faces
blurting "yes" and a lover flat
enough for a wallet,

raising her value to a full boast.
The heat of her Monday breath
spread across schoolyard girls,
The air of her world rising. ❧

Portrait #24

Clarence Shelley

The halls are empty now.
I feel
a deep, uneasy loneliness:
Who will protect my children from the street
and from each other,
from themselves?
It would be idiocy to believe
that Robert's ready to face three o'clock and after
armed only with the book he will not read;
that poetry and pronouns
will keep Gwen from getting pregnant
before Monday brings her home to me.
It's been a good day for this time and place:
Ray argued with me,
Mary found an error I had left for her
and showed it to me.
Yet, fumbling for my keys, I find
I cannot read the unimportant scrawls
that made the blackboard real
an hour ago. I turn the light out,
lock the door.
It is time to go.

Playing Scrabble with Eddie

Taylor Mali

Despite his dyslexia, or perhaps because of it,
Eddie can beat every other eighth grader in Scrabble.
Kick their ass in fact, and he knows it,
though he can't say it, at least not in those words,
because if he said "ass" in my eighth grade
I'd give him detention on the spot.

Scrabble was made for his mind.
Show him a rack of seven letters,
he'll tell you in an instant ten different words
that use some combination of those letters,
his mind is hardwired for confusion,
for discombobulating vowels
and the jangling clangor of consonants.
But ask him to spell those ten words,
and he may DARE to READ DEAR
when the word READS DREAD.

Combine dyslexia with hyperactivity,
which now we call ADD,
Attention Deficit Disorder,
though Eddie says impishly, DDA!
Fifteen milligrams of Ritalin taken twice a day,
dispensed by the nurse, an IQ of 165,
and all the hormones of a thirteen-year-old boy
dying for an education, and you have
one horny, whacked-out, eighth-grade genius
staring at the seven tiles on his rack
as if only getting the letters in the right order
would unlock all the secrets of the language.

Eddie stares at my face, at the board, at his rack,
at his rack, at the board, at my face.
And I wonder what his dyslexic, rearranging mind

is doing with my eyes and my ears and my nose.
How many one-eyed, Picasso-faced English teachers
Are staring back at him from the educated audience of his adolescence?
But here comes the word:

    K-C-U-F

KCUF? Eddie, I think I'm going to have to challenge you on this word.
And Eddie reddens. Eddie reddens
like he finally got the punch line to a dirty joke,
which in a way he has. Eddie reddens
like I've finally caught him swearing,
which in a way I haven't. Yet.

And the letters pivot around the K.

    C-U-F.

Oh. Fuck! Well, that's different.

    "Is that okay, Mr. Mali?"

Is that okay!? Is that okay, Eddie!?
You landed the F on a double letter square
and the K on a double word!
That's 34 points, young man!

    "Hot shit!" says Eddie.

And I give him a detention on the spot. 🙿

Eric

Peggy Raines

—for Terry and other grieving mothers

Each day, she must be asking
    Where did my son go?
Her smooth-faced beautiful boy
        the popular athlete
        the polite adolescent
        the good student

        into the paranoia
        glazed eyes
        outside the lines
        beyond reason

Who is this person
        standing accused of
        pulling the trigger
        ending a policeman's life
        living inside steel bars
        deep in despair
        away from her?

Who is he? ᘚ

The Results of Some Hoping

Maryfrances Wagner

Ardith, last in line down the steps, is the only student
lugging books in a fire drill. Like a bird,
she tilts her head at me the same way
her mother, Lydia, did twenty years ago,
when we were students here. Red-headed Lydia
sputtered and wheezed whenever she raised a hand,
all of us shifting, setting down our pens, some hoping
she'd raise those eyes above clusters of used tissues,
afloat on her desk like wilted gardenias.
Although I untangled her from hooks and latches,
I wished just once she'd open her locker
on the first try, not call out for me to wait.
Lydia, the only girl unable to run a lap, dribble a ball,
the single pep squad member waving a crew-sweatered arm
among cheering V-necks, the lone girl stumbling
down bus aisles, snagging her spiral on jackets,
missing the last step, the easiest equation.
When Ardith reaches the door,
she leans into her sliding geometry book.
Everything tumbles like a bad juggling act.
A pencil and highlighter bounce off her elbow.
We shoo her into open air,
scramble for books fluttering behind her.
As she measures the last step with a toe,
her red hair spirals in the wind;
a flurry of Kleenex lifts from her purse like doves. 🙰

Stepping Out

Sara Holbrook

—for the Bay Village
High School class of 1993

The world made room for you, babies,
your toothless grins and charms.
Clapped when you took first steps
and held you in privileged arms.

Such a magical reception!
Trees turned into cribs
and diapers and announcements.
"Violá!" exclaimed the world.
"These babies will need bibs,
and vitamins and formula
and pint-sized tube socks for their toes.
These babies will need central heat.
These babies," it said.
"Not those."

Presto! Pigs turned into hot dogs.
Cows into burgers and sneaker leather.
Geese and sheep gave up their coats
to protect you from Cleveland weather.
Water turned into colas.
Potatoes into chips.
Rocks turned into fuel
to propel you on your trips
to malls and work and school.

And then, the world taxed
all your neighbors
so you could learn, but secondhand,
all about starvation,
about deprivation,
about dictators and
war.

The goblins of the world,
viewed through a media peephole
in a sturdy suburban door.

We know.
No one asked you if this was fair,
to be raised on top-shelf milk.
The world will ask you for answers,
but the question is not guilt.
It's privilege.
Is it just a blessing?
A responsibility?
A maze of social traps?
An isolationist position?
Or is it just, perhaps,
a gilded invitation to help
construct a place
where less is more,
where more costs less
and where more babies can be safe?

The world made room for you,
when it was crowded and hungry and tired,
hoping, one day, that comfort
would grow uncomfortable.
That one day you'd grow
inspired to find solutions.
The world gave you the strength
to seek that "something else,"
and to stand up to
the nonchalance of privilege
as now, you step out
to make room for yourself. &

Teachers' Poetry about
THEIR INNER LIVES

INTRODUCTION

Teachers' Poetry
about Their Inner Lives

Margaret Hatcher

Be faithful to that which exists nowhere but in yourself.
—André Gide

It seems to be a universal experience where teachers are concerned. It happens anytime and anywhere . . . supermarkets, movie theaters, shopping malls, restaurants, public restrooms, airports, any public place, really. It goes like this: I am in the produce section of my favorite supermarket, engrossed in the avocado I am squeezing, and a voice, stunned and slightly thrilled, will ring out: "Ms. Hatcher! What are YOU doing HERE?!" As if teachers live on light or pure air and never leave their classrooms!

Or I am having dinner with a friend, and a voice, all business and full of its own concerns, cuts into my main entrée and dinner conversation with: "Dr. Hatcher, excuse me, but you need to know that Johnny came home from school today and said . . ." As if a teacher's time is a part of the public domain. Or I am leaving a movie, concentrating on adjusting my eyes to the sunlight, and behind me a voice will sing out: "Ms. Hatcher! Didn't Luke Skywalker remind you of *The Red Badge of Courage* when he said . . ." As if teachers never escape their curriculum, as if we have no interests outside our subject areas. Every teacher can tell you experiences such as these.

How do we explain this? Very simply, it seems that, unlike members of any other profession, teachers are perceived, not only by their students, but also by the general public, primarily as educators rather than as human beings. No matter what endeavor we pursue, we all seem to struggle with the balance between our personal, inner lives and our professional lives. For teachers, this struggle is especially challenging, not only because of others' perceptions, but also because of the nature of teachers and the nature of our profession. Teaching is all-consuming because, for most of us, it is a calling and not just a job. And so we breathe it, sleep and wake with it, walk and sit with it . . . live it.

Research shows that the very best, most powerful, and inspiring teachers, the teachers who are human beings and not just academics, are those whose inner, personal lives are as rich as their intellectual, academic, and professional lives. Indeed the personal life deepens, enriches, informs, and inspires the professional life, and vice versa. For it is in the inner life that the real wisdom of teachers is gained and is expressed; it is in the inner life that the dispositions, or habits of mind and heart that make teachers great, as opposed to mediocre technicians, are born and nurtured.

Consider the most powerful and influential teachers in your life. Consider the qualities and attributes that made them such to you. Inevitably, we respond with something like: That teacher really woke me up, or inspired me, or got hold of my mind, or was the first to believe in me and help me believe in myself. We express it in different ways, but however we say it, we are talking about teachers' inner qualities of character, such as integrity, authenticity, compassion, passion, patience, honesty, sense of humor.

Few teachers are remembered for their impact on our lives because of knowing about the difference between a nominative absolute and an indirect object, or because of how skillfully they taught us to manipulate algebraic equations, or because of how dramatically they engaged us in the drama of the Civil War. No, teachers' impact and inspiration come primarily from the persons they are, from their hearts, courage, integrity, caring, enthusiasm, quickness, passion and spirit, and perspective on the world, and secondarily from the ideas and skills they teach. Indeed, great teachers do, as Rumi says, "Let the beauty they love be what they do." Vibrant and spirited teachers are true to, nurture, and explore that which exists nowhere but within themselves. They use these inner resources as deep reserves for the spirit and passion that pervade their teaching.

And so, this section of poetry focuses on these personal and inner reservoirs of teachers, their loves, pleasures, joys, dreams, fears, creativity, losses, grief, ambiguities, and doubts. In celebration of all of us who walk the path of teacher, may the poems that follow in this section bring us new insights about our own inner lives; remind us of our own critical moments of joy, challenge, fear, courage, and compassion; inspire us to live balanced, whole, conscious lives; and reward us for all that we have done and been in the lives of our students and our loved ones, as well as for all that we have done for our own growth, health, spirit, and well-being. ❧

CONTENTS OF THIS SECTION

CONTENTS OF THIS SECTION _(continued)_

On Watching Jenny Go Too Fast

Rex Grove

She was six that summer—
that summer of purple swimming suits
   and orange Popsicles and sleeping bag
   overnights at Matt's house.
It was that summer that she outgrew
our family favorite loop-around-the-neighborhood
   bike ride
and asked me, could she ride alone.
Worry tinged my uh-I-guess-so
   as she rode off, turning to give me her smug smile
   before I had a chance to reconsider.
And then one day she flipped me an invitation to go along.
She set the pace, careening down a bumpy hill, dodging potholes,
   her handlebars jerking in girl-child hands,
but she, intent and eager, somehow stayed on course.
Father-like, I wanted to yell at her: You've got to slow down!
   You've got to be careful!

But, catching myself, I knew—even then—
   that was only the beginning of Jenny's wanting to go faster
   and of my wanting her to go carefully. ❦

Tightrope Walking at Fifty-Four

Sally M. Oran

I've been lost before
Along these borders.
You'd think I'd learn my way.

At nine I avoided the cracks
That break mothers' backs
And searched sidewalk edges
Of clover clumps down Fifth Street
For five-leafed rarities:
City-girl medicine.

At seventeen I balanced the measure
Of invite and deny
And held enough power
For a multitude of Masai matriarchs,
Or one single black mother:
Adolescent electricity.

At twenty-two I gambled the odds
Of wait and want
And found satisfaction enough
To carry me over the boundary
To thirty-six and face death:
Square in the eye.

Since then I have lived in margins
That have become
My mainstream.
I am a negative image
In a dusky darkroom awaiting solutions:
A perfect word portrait.

I'm tightrope walking at fifty-four,
Unbalanced on the wire
And trembling in thin air.
Is it any wonder the world is upside down
And I see the sky as a great
Ocean breaking on the tops of trees?

I've fallen before
From these edges.
You'd think I'd learn.

Chemotherapy
Maryfrances Wagner

Up from bed after three days,
you reach for a curl to twist.
It drops in your hand.
Your other tightens on my arm.
I lean beside you,
rest my cheek next to yours.
We are quiet like the snow outside.
We watch cardinals spill seed from the feeder.
I mention they've lived here a long time;
you tell me you miss the wrens.
I think of when I straddled the chair
to brush the hair I loved to touch,
the hair where I buried my head
to find the familiar curve in your neck.

Today your hair drops
after twenty strokes
into the sack
waiting under the brush.
I rub the smooth pink egg
your head has become,
hold you tight
as you always held me.
Outside it is cold.
We spend the afternoon
combing and recombing a wig,
trying to find the place inside us
where we know this doesn't matter,
waiting to talk until we do.

Barbara at Forty-Five

Roselyn Young

You look in the mirror and see only:
stomach;
it is too round, too fat.
With the loathing
reserved for a snake
in the garden
you slap at it
and cram it
into panty hose.
You mourn age
with the false edge of
every magazine page.
Restless hands
on your stomach,
you miss the sleek
hipbones of your
daughters.

I look in the mirror and see only:
you;
you have a woman's belly
filled three times
with children
who curled like
kittens under your
good heart.
Celebrate experience
with every smooth turn
of the calendar.
Rest your hands on
your daughters;
feel the soft rise
of your own full
life. ❧

Pieces of a Country Childhood

Marion Razler

When I was little,
And the scabs on my knees a
Permanent condition,
I used to promise God
That I'd be really good if
He'd let me run across the
Gravel drive just once—
Without falling.
That was in the dusty, red-gold season
When the hickory dropped its fruit,
And I would get my fingers sticky
Pulling green velvet covers
Off the hazelnuts. I picked
Blackberries in the hills, and pulled
Long pods off the old catalpa.

Now a concrete river has drowned
The fields, but let me tell you
I can still taste the stain of wild berries on my
      lips,
And when I walk on gravel,
My knees hurt. ❧

To Father

Angela M. Maloy

Your hands came home each night
smelling like wood,
their brown-carved music
smooth as moondust.
Carla and I,
we moved a maple rhythm
in that winter kitchen,
breathing in your day
of pine and cypress.
The shavings hung in layers
from our ears;
we were a Gypsy's daughters
barefoot in sawdust,
twirling under a yellow bulb.
Supper warmed our faces.

Now you are dead,
your hands themselves turned wood.
Crouched in line behind that box,
we are sick of mums
and uncles in brown suits
whose buttons mark our cheeks.

And who will clap on Monday
when we dance? &

Remind Me

Donna Cooner

Remind me again
why this is better.
Remind me
why this has to be.
Remind me.

Because I remember
talking every night to someone
who cared how my day went.
I remember dancing barefoot in the living room,
I remember laughing,
I remember someone who loved the way
my nose wrinkled up
when he touched it.

I remember sleeping sometimes
with him curled warmly against my back,
his arms wrapped tightly around my waist,
his breathing deep against my hair.

I remember . . . things.

So remind me again why this is better
—this choice I've made—
This life of silence and isolation
filled with cold sheets and empty tables,
where no one touches me,
except to shake my hand.
Remind me why.

I always forget. ▰

Thomasdancing

Daniel Henry

You are just three months old
as I move around the bedroom
trying to put you
to sleep before dinner;
You have other ideas.
I'm trying to remember
how simple this is:
How in this moment
all choices are between
sleeping and crying;
I wonder if you
will ever believe
you were carried,
so easily in my arms:
Years from now
when we move
in other steps
we cannot even imagine—
will you remember,
somewhere in your bones,
that I sang
"Stardust" to you?
Will this be
the love letter found
in the attic
of our anger
when you are grown
and too far away?

Spirit Song
Margaret Hatcher

Riding the earth
      past the stars,
I spent my Self
      hiding
      the shadows inside me,
      telling
          all the stories
          except the ones I was living,
      looking back,
          then forward,
      listening
          to a voice and
      trying
          to be what it said,
      becoming
          me, lost in my own crystal story.
Then
      by grace and mystery
      a parachute opens and jerks,
      and suddenly
I know I've been falling
      for years . . .
And I finally see:

I am part
      of this infinite dream
          and
      the hardest war to fight
          is the one
          you don't know
          you're in. ❧

Depth Finder

Maryfrances Wagner

I can't see my husband from the study,
but I know he's at the window looking out,
thinking as he waters the hibiscus.
He loves the silence of his plants
reaching up, new blooms like offerings.
I know he's watching the wind
dipping and lifting the leaves outside.
He knows about wind and direction,
about feeding his sails so his boat
leans and skims towards the dam.
He says little as he stares across the lake,
as though he's listening to the wind's
breath and his own become one.
He needs only a depth finder so we
don't go aground. This is my job,
to monitor depth. At times, I pull
winch ropes. Tonight I hear the water
soaking the plants, the wind setting off
the chimes. I join my husband where
he stares out the window. Sometimes
when I stand on the bow as he glides us
into the cove, I can almost touch what he feels. ❧

Avoiding the Poem

Kim Holland

The lengths I go to avoid the poem
the bathtub has been sandblasted
the back fence painted
every square inch of dirt hoed, weeded, planted.
I would thin the ponderosas
I would skin the surreal cerulean blue sky
I would pick a fight
Indulge in literary criticism.
I would eat almost anything in the refrigerator
Watch almost anybody on the television
Call almost anyone on the phone
To avoid memory
To avoid injury
To avoid mystery.

I'm not alone. I've seen you early morning
rushing to avoid dreams' shadows,
eating lunch in herds to kill solitude,
packing each hour with lists and mission statements.
It is a growth industry—
avoiding the poem.
It lasts for years. Think of all the newspapers,
games of golf, new clothes, miles logged.
It takes skill, makeup, plastic surgery,
soft lights, and the kindness of strangers
to keep up the pretense that
what we do is necessary.

I remember, once after surgery,
my face not yet mended,
one side smiled—the other didn't,
and one eye continually cried.
It disturbed my students
who thought I was terminal
or at least schizophrenic. "The proportion

will grow back," the doctor promised. But it didn't.
There is a hollow here. It is my personalized metaphor.
It is me: so timid, so afraid.
It sweats when I eat.

This year I was taught to recognize anorexia.
A telling sign is tooth enamel.
Beautiful young girls' teeth
are furry brown, and the bird bones
of their long arms seem almost blue.
They look in the mirror
but they can't see their faces;
they see taut balloons ready to burst.
The only cure is patience. One father's
daughter began to disappear when she was seventeen.
He sold the house, quit his job,
and whisked her away to the ocean.
I think of him sitting on the sand
rocking her in his arms—
and she is as light as the child of his memory.

I know that this is not that,
but it is difficult to know what sustains
and what destroys. Words are not easy.
I move them with my tongue
feeling their shape,
and I don't want to swallow.
I pick them out with my fingers
look at them—slimy and disgusting
stringy green like chewed asparagus—
This is not what I imagined at all.

Isn't all hollowness related?
Like birds we seek what is essential
before we slam startled against the window.
It is easy to panic.
I am forgetting words, images, stories.
The people who knew the answers are dead or silent.
I am afraid. Will I die choking
or starved? ❧

This Makes Me Strong

Sally M. Oran

This makes me strong:
To give like the wind
Who lifts the eagle wing and
Tiny seed alike aloft
Not for those purposes but
As a generous gesture of identity
On her homeward path.

This makes me strong:
To be honest like the rain
Who shapeshifts from cloud to mist
To the quiet course of bloodwater
As she fulfills her purpose
In a million forms, every one for
Life and strength and spirit.

This makes me strong:
To choose life as my classroom
Using every dimension
To learn and live and grow
Counterbalanced in my own
Unique rhythm and harmony
Poised ready to dance and be.

This makes me strong:
To align my spirit with my own truth
By speaking it continually to my eyes
And testing the measure of pace
And direction and fixing
My bearings by my own lodestar.

This makes me strong:
To refuse safety just for comfort
Or rest or giving up; I will remind

Myself of new channels rivers make when
Their strength surges and their
Life becomes a torrent of power.

This makes me strong:
To reside in music every day and
Tune my thoughts to old refrains
And new lyrics in liquid
Languages of melody that
Instruct my soul to sing.

This makes me strong:
To speak my "no" when I feel unsafe;
To rely on myself to mind the boundaries
I require others to obey and in
Doing so keep my soul's custody
And recite my body's refuge.

This makes me strong:
To circumscribe open range
As the space for your wandering
While speaking the dangers of
Low washes and high mesas
And declaring my heart the chamber
Where you whisper and remove your shoes. &

To Denise Pelan

Andrew Green

The most beautiful girl in seventh grade
who turned me down
when I asked her to a dance,
simply said, "No way,"
and that in front of twenty pals
who wouldn't let me forget it
the rest of the year.

It's true I was skinny, had too many pimples,
and quite frankly, had no business asking her.
But still, "No way, no way?"
A simple "no" would have sufficed.
An excuse would have been better:
"I've already got plans" perhaps,
or "We're going away that weekend."

Anything, anything at all,
but those were earlier days, Denise,
over twenty years ago. We've since grown up.

Denise, may your golden hair turn the color of bacon fat
may your pearly whites buck up to the heavens
and may those long brown legs
      reach a state of varicosity
      that makes the Himalayas
      look like a baby's tush. &

My Bones, My Life

Peggy Raines

Grandmothers, sing over my bones as they
glisten white and sterile in the moonlight,
lying on the sand, by the lake's edge,
scattered, disconnected, disjointed . . .

How do we become so fragmented?
How does the connective tissue of our life become so stretched?
Years, miles, ages pass, and we rattle along . . .
Our minds race, our souls wither . . .

Guide me, Grandmothers,
breathe life into my heart,
sing me awake.
Hold me in your soft warm arms.
Smile your snaggle-toothed grins,
and remind me of my beauty, my gifts . . .

Mend my ragged nerves, rock me,
lift me toward the stars,
shimmering sisters of the universe,
and free me from my fear. ❧

Mother

Kelly Joe Pagnac

I sit across from my mother in a café
sharing a sandwich.

After each bite her pink, painted lips
twitch, setting her jaw into a rhythmic motion

that reels me back
into the Sundays of my childhood

when she lay in bed,
long past noon,

those same lips twitching,
that same masticating jaw;

only it's depression she's chewing on,
biting off big chunks from that

crusty loaf of melancholy—
digesting the blunt parasite of

grief and woe that breeds without discretion
and feasts between the cracks and fissures

of her genetic sidewalk. Once again
her words fill up my ears,

slip a knot inside my throat.
She's cursing my father, blaming him for

those little shits who drowned her dreams
in the Dead Sea of motherhood,

those little shits who sealed her future
in an empty box, then buried it in a place

where there is no X and nothing
marks the spot. I want to tell her

those little shits
had ears—instead, I reach over and wipe

the mustard from her cheek. 🔖

154

Tasting the Word

Judy Michaels

And now these guys want to raise a child
together. All afternoon I've bitched
about my mother, and they've bitched about theirs.
One of them was my student once,
grubby and hyper: He had to own my class,
talked us to death. (The word "gay"
fluttered around his head, just out of reach.
At night it roosted in corners.)

Now home is the futon where his lover
brushes sleep and blond curls from his eyes.
Up late reunifying Germany,
He's hungry for angelhair and peppers.
He slips in their favorite tape,
lights candles, and plays that he's cooking
cereal for the two-year-old. Both dream
of the little girl who hugs their waist each time
they visit Case 3214. Things aren't so good there.
The foster mother drinks a lot. They picture
bruises, and bathing that small body,
talcum between the toes . . .

How much of "parenthood" is fantasy, anyway?
Just a word. I float it off my tongue
as I help them clean up. The word drifts
into the suds, a little wafer of light
losing itself in steam. But it sounds heavy,
like German. "Is your child in order?"
I once read on a sign there.
Are we in order? What if I had two fathers?
My tongue flicks my teeth—fathers—the final
growl and hiss. But they are gentle
together. From them I might have learned
generosity and to say what I want.
To be brave with power tools and strangers.
They are makers and healers,
and better at child's play than I,
though mothers still sing in our sleep. &

Giant Clown

Maryfrances Wagner

When I called mother
to my bed late at night,
she insisted,
"There's no clown at your window."
His painted frown,
his tapping, gloved hands,
his polka-dot tie
haunted my nights
where I tried, under a flood of sweat,
eyes squeezed tight, to lie still
until he went away.

At six, my nephew,
sheet tugged to his eyes,
called me to his bed.
"A giant clown at my window."
"There's no clown,"
I started, then bit those words.
"He's got a rifle and a polka-dot tie."
"Where?"
"Right there," he pointed.
"Wanna sleep in my room?" I asked.

When mother started killing cancer pain
with methadone, she was certain
elves built puppets at night across the street,
cows stomped through the house.
"Those things aren't really there,"
I insisted. "It's just the medicine."
One afternoon she added,
"Last night I saw a giant clown
outside the window."
"A clown?" I asked.
"What did he look like?"

Unforgotten Lessons: Remembered

James Hobbs

I know a poem I have written and given out to
my teacher friends has hit home when they
turn out of their classrooms, like generals
clearing their tents, to come to my classroom
to say such things as: "You and I must have
had the same mother!" "You must have gone
to school when I did." "There are so many
things we used to do that you used to do!"
And I do enjoy the smiles on our faces, and
I get to hear so many wonderful stories.

The poem is like a dropped handkerchief, and
here they come, and we stand in open classroom
doors, oblivious to students trooping in, and
we live our school days, and we forget
for a moment that we are teachers as we reach
that reserve that probably brought us the love
of family and to teaching in the first place.

Moon-Chasing

Sally M. Oran

I went moon-chasing tonight—
A promise I made to myself in the cold of a starless winter night
When my internal magnet seemed to go awry
And I was lost.

That January I had longed to see canyon walls
Mirror the moon on a pine-scented night,
Imagining that combination a
Medicine and map for my spirit.

So I went moon-chasing tonight—
I swayed in the splendor on the canyon rim
With my arms outstretched and my palms heavenward, and
I swear I could taste the moon's breath.

I lost myself to the night's power and
Submitted myself to the same claws of moonlight and clime
That rake downward through the canyon trees and rocks
And expose the soul of that place.

I went moon-chasing tonight—
And beneath the arc of the rising full moon
The tide of my contentment surged and stilled and
Aligned with all of night. ❧

Sunday's Child

Nancy V. Swanson

If he wears a Braves cap at dinner
and leaves Popsicle papers and sticks
strewn across the floor, she doesn't mind.

He's sixteen, and it's probably her fault
anyway for not making him say yes
ma'am, not requiring him to mow the
lawn, not scowling at *shit* or *damn*. Anyway
he stacks dishes when asked and allows
her to laugh at his Nike shirts. Lately,
he's developed a Marlboro-man muscle
twitch in his left cheek and talks
to her about chemistry and baseball
games and music. The point is, you
can't claim him after his foot
no longer fits in the palm of your
hand. Any teenage girl can
tell you that. Put aside the rules
you should have had, the Dylan songs
he doesn't like, the closed door to his room.

Think of long-fingered hands that open
jars, that rest easy on a steering wheel. See,
after all these years of letting go, where
he takes himself. 🍃

On Contemplating Resignation

Deena Hardin

Maybe it's just me, but looking out
at a sea of young, inquisitive faces
wanting to know what I know
makes me tired, so tired.
Surely the oracles retired nightly
in a completely spent condition.
Worst thing about it, for me,
is that I don't feel human all day,
that I feel like a *teacher*,
an oracle maybe, function like one,
then have to go home and be human,
oh, so human (laundry and cooking
and cleaning and getting kids to bed
are certainly things oracles didn't do).
What the hell. Oracles were things
people made up because they lacked
teachers or a broad base of knowledge—
a *mythology*, of course, is what it was,
like those myths about teachers'
short days and great vacation packages.

Saturday Mornings

Margaret Hatcher

I love to stretch like this
        in my bed on Saturday mornings,
        simply listening . . .

I know all the dark places
        where the sun hasn't reached yet:
                anthills where the movement is unceasing,
                sleeping spiders, dreaming of spinning.
I hear a butterfly stirring
        deep within a caterpillar,
        and the earth dreaming of warm, quiet rain.
Somewhere a stone cracks open,
        another turns in its sleep,
And I hear the grass singing
        its green wet song . . .
And all of a sudden
        in the midst of it all
                it seems possible

        to learn
        to teach
                and to live

        simply
        here and now
        on this earth. &

The Women with Accents

Renee Ruderman

I should have listened to them
dressed in their German accents
and stockinged, husky legs.
I would have heard their songs
about reading to absorb the night,
how the wind whisked their coats
open on New York City's dark corners.

They were grateful for my mother's invitations;
came out on the train, breathed in green hills,
but they were never too hungry,
lifting forks slowly, curving their words
over goulash, smiling at me like hands
taking me where I did not want to go.

"Yes, I have a boyfriend," I told her.
"*Nicht du!*" she shook her head,
tucking it into her neck.
They admired my youth
and combed it into my vanity.
I forgot to ask, "What did you have
To leave behind?" and
"What happened to your husband?"

I edged toward the door;
Drove top-down, cross-town. 🍃

For Barbara, on the Death of Her Student

Roselyn Young

Mourn in the yard with the snapdragons
because none of it makes any sense:
not the weeping of the trees,
not the peeling of the paint,
not the tilt of the fence.

Find something that can be repaired:
the lawn that needs edging,
the hedge that needs clipping,
separate the weeds from the strawberries,
and let the ripe fruit
pour into your apron.

For now anyway
you can't even hurt a fly,
but cup its frightened buzzing
between your palms
and set it somewhere
gently.

Salute

Maryfrances Wagner

I slit the last bag
of father's crappie,
let the odor sift up
from the sink,
an imprint
of his last summers,
when he sandwiched walking
and meals together
around fishing.
The freezer date,
markered in his even print,
now fading like a watercolor,
was only a month
before my uncle found him—
his face still pink
when I arrived,
no different than Sundays
when he napped,
his flat fingers
interlaced across his chest.
My uncle covered him with a blanket
while I stood waiting
as though any minute
he might open his eyes.
Only hours before
we had tapped wineglasses,
salute,
shared antipasto and linguini,
hugged good-byes before I drove away.
Now I cover the white fillets
with tarragon, lemon, dill,
enough for two to eat. ❦

Between the Lines

Ruth Trowbridge

Don't tell me again that one day
Prince Charming will arrive.
I remember all those fairy tales—
Only too well.
Who could take seriously
Some guy who'd spend half his life
Searching for thornless roses in the snow?
Or traveling east of the sun and west of the moon?
Or trying to climb glass mountains?
His reward is to marry the fair princess
(Whose opinion is never asked)
And live happily ever after.

But what about the princess?
What's her reward?
He gets to quaff mead with his cronies,
Open parliament,
And show everyone the picture of him
Standing on the dragon's head.
She gets to keep a drafty castle clean,
Plan the banquets,
Have the babies,
And keep from screaming every time someone
        says,
"Is your husband *the* Prince Charming?
You lucky girl!"

Personally, I'd rather wait for Rumpelstiltskin,
At least, he'll expect me to think.

Transformation

Peggy Raines

I feel the breath of Skeleton Woman when
the wind howls through the ponderosas
and my house shudders and shifts.

Late, late in the night, alone in the darkness,
I move deeper under the soft down comforter
and begin the night dramas
that are so often my companions,
my dreams, my stories.

She speaks to me in the form of Sister Eagle or Gray Wolf,
and sometimes Bear turns and faces me
with a new and often frightening message.

They tell me their stories, they guide and protect me
and, at times, they shake my belief,
they rattle my bones, and they change me.

I awaken to the tremors of transformation,
the movement of my spirit.

But then, rather suddenly, the sun's light
and the cry of my old, crotchety cat
bring me out of the womb of sleep
to a more jangling and hectic reality.

But if only I would take that spirit time
during my harried day to remember . . .
I know that Skeleton Woman touched me in the night
and breathed a difference into my woman soul. 🔹

Half-Light

Gail Peck

When the change hit my grandmother
she did nothing but stare
into a mirror
while my grandfather took over
the cooking and cleaning.
Not a vain woman, but attractive.
What thoughts reflected there?
Perhaps all the sad things returned:
her infant boy who smothered
sleeping beside her, the son
whose car ran off the road one night
and all that was left was gambling money.
It was the only time I saw my grandmother cry—
the state troopers in the doorway
with their badges and their guns.

I don't know when my grandmother
picked up her life again,
began polishing the stove
and playing Jim Reeves on the record player.
She started cleaning houses for people,
ruining some things with Clorox,
and after my grandfather's death
fell in love once more. Though I think
it was really the habit of caring for someone,
the way a woman I knew
continued setting two places at the table
after her husband died, and sat down
across from the vacant chair.

Desert Disciple

Sally M. Oran

I cast a covenant with this demanding desert
To be her disciple, thus
Obligating myself
To a certain devotion and
Obedience.

Little knowing I would witness her sure seasons
I entered her amber
Moods in willing wonder,
Imprinting her aromas on
My memory.

She drew me to her like an artistic tutor
And I walked her lessons
And mastered her sand themes;
I laid her lyrics to my own mystical music—
Sienna symphony.

She called me to her promises and great, wide washes
Winding near the heart roots
Of silent silver cottonwoods
Knee-deep in patience and still sand—
Awaiting water.

And then I learned the very hardest lesson
Of all her storied dunes and droughts.
A sovereign astride wind
She brandished a chisel and carved
Stone chronicles.

Brutal beauty, this raking insult to rearrange
Stone in a ritual
That indelibly marks
A noble contoured countenance
With saffron scars.

I stand in the frightful face of my desert teacher
While her west-wind talons
Etch huge urgent archives
In terrible tattoos,
And I am converted—sanctioned
With her signature. ✍

Mask-Making in a Farmhouse Kitchen

Maryfrances Wagner

Clustered, we waited
for wet plaster strips
to cover Vaselined faces
until we were voiceless,
trapped in a facial moment
we might never pose again,
incubating, somewhere
where there were no faces,
until cool fingers
lifted away a shell of ourselves.

We set white faces
to harden in the sun,
faces that drew us back
to stare, to touch
the hard, white cheek.

When we tried them on,
one said the early people of Jericho
called them death masks,
spirits trapped in faces.
Another said artists
call them life masks,
faces' exact images.
At home, I hang mine
in the window.
Against the morning backlight,
it stares back at me,
a stranger
from every angle,
a hidden self,
even when I try it on. ❧

The Lesson

Susan Patton

A professor once told a story about a truck driver
who spotted a corrugated box in a street.
Rather than leave it to harm others
he drove over it, only to discover
two children playing inside.

With this, he explained
the importance of surprise endings.

Thirty years later,
I read the last page
of every book first.

The Dance

Marty Williams

When she turned thirteen
my daughter kept a bird.
Water and fresh seed,
daily gestures, taught her
something of love, the tiny bones
gentleness, the bright
eye quickness of being.

The bird died suddenly.
My daughter, refusing ritual,
tucks in upon herself,
an emptiness in the middle,
the heart's nest.

From the side, I watch my daughter
rehearse a dance. The children move
together, first this arm
a wing, then the other.
The teacher calls, "Smoothly now,
make me forget you have feet,
make me believe you can fly."

My daughter dances,
chest unfolded to the skies,
that broad, smooth way
birds do, lifting, dipping,
slantwise to life.

Patchwork Poems

Evelyn Wood Lawery

My mother-in-law's poems
Are made with little scraps of cloth,
From a generation of party dresses,
           neckties, and work clothes,
Bits of life sewn in similes and metaphors.
           The party dress is like a star.
           The necktie is a rose.
           The work clothes are country fences.
She names them:
                   Star of Texas
                   Rose of Sharon
                   Rail Fence
Her sons and daughters carry them
           away in dowry chests,
And on cold winter nights,
Wrapped in her extended metaphors,
           They make grandchildren. 🐦

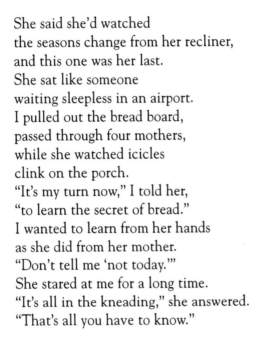

The Importance of Kneading

Maryfrances Wagner

She said she'd watched
the seasons change from her recliner,
and this one was her last.
She sat like someone
waiting sleepless in an airport.
I pulled out the bread board,
passed through four mothers,
while she watched icicles
clink on the porch.
"It's my turn now," I told her,
"to learn the secret of bread."
I wanted to learn from her hands
as she did from her mother.
"Don't tell me 'not today.'"
She stared at me for a long time.
"It's all in the kneading," she answered.
"That's all you have to know."

I sifted, warmed yeast with water,
waited in silence with her
while the dough breathed
and seeped over the bowl.
"Punch it down," she spoke,
never having checked a clock.
I buried my hands into the warm mound,
pushed down with the heel of my palm,
over and down, over and down,
until I found the rhythm,
the dough springing back
supple as young skin.

"You'll know by the feel," she called to me.
"Then you'll never forget;
you'll always make good bread."

174

She scooted on slippers into the kitchen
when I told her I thought it was time,
still not sure what I had to feel.
Her hands sunk in next to mine.
We pushed together
like the times we played duets on the piano.
"There," she said at last,
and I saw in her eyes
what Father said was always alive.

CREDITS

For permission to reproduce copyrighted material in this book, the author and publisher gratefully acknowledge the following (copyright and permission to print by author unless otherwise acknowledged):

Atkinson, Charles: "Composition," "With Apologies"

Balaban, Camille: "A Morning Like This" from *English Journal*, Jan. 1992 (© 1992 by the National Council of Teachers of English, hereafter abbreviated NCTE)

Baron, Kathi: "Absolution by Teacher," "Kids"

Benson, Laura: "Dance"

Berkley, June Langford: "Lines for Ms. Margaret (1922–99)"

Bottaccini, Manfred: "Miss Brower Joins the Marines"

Bratcher, Suzanne: "Ganado Trading Post"

Callaway, Melissa: "For Ronald"

Chafin, Shirley R.: "Cycles" from *English Journal*, Oct. 1982 (© 1982 NCTE)

Connolly, J. F.: "Telling My Sister How I Taught a Lesson on Child Abuse" from *English Journal*, Sept. 1992 (© 1992 NCTE)

Cooner, Donna: "Remind Me"

Draper, Sharon: "Band-Aids and Five-Dollar Bills"

Dunaway, Samantha: "To a Sleeping High-School Student, or Sweet Oblivion" from *English Journal*, Jan. 1999 (© 1999 NCTE)

Fehler, Gene: "Cal Norris" from *English Journal*, Mar. 1991 (© 1991 NCTE)

Ferri, Daniel: "Backwards Day," "Carrying Water," "Elbows"; "Backwards Day" first appeared in *Poetry Slam: The Competitive Art of Performance Poetry* (Manic D 2000)

Goldsmith, Karyl: "Students"

Green, Andrew: "To Denise Pelan" from *English Journal*, Oct. 1994 (© 1994 NCTE)

Grove, Rex: "On Watching Jenny Go Too Fast" from *English Journal*, Jan. 1983 (© 1983 NCTE)

Hardin, Deena: "On Contemplating Resignation"

Hatcher, Margaret: "Forced Entry: To My Students, with Love," "On My First Year of Teaching," "Saturday Mornings," "Spirit Song," "A Teaching Fantasy," "To Walt Whitman"

Henry, Daniel: "Thomasdancing" from *English Journal*, Mar. 1993 (© 1993 NCTE)

Hicks, Jean W.: "Body Language"

Hillmer, Timothy: "For a Student, on Leaving Seventh Grade"

Hobbs, James: "Teacher Review," "Unforgotten Lessons: Remembered"; "Teacher Review" first appeared in *The Primer*, Spring/Summer 2000

Holbrook, Sara: "Free Lunch," "Stepping Out," "Whooping It up at the MTV Saloon"

Holland, Kim: "Avoiding the Poem"

Inclan, Jessica Barksdale: "A Charm in His Arms," "Mi Palomita," "Something We Can Hold"

Johnson, Theresa: "Dear Mr. District Superintendent" from *English Journal*, Mar. 1983 (© 1983 NCTE)

Lamm, C. Drew: "Teacher Me Sweet" from *English Journal*, Jan. 1990 (© 1990 NCTE)

Lawery, Evelyn Wood: "Patchwork Poems" from *English Journal*, May 1977 (© 1977 NCTE)

Loewe, Ron: "Dark Nights" from *English Journal*, May 1979 (© 1979 NCTE)

Lynch, Kathleen: "The Boy" from *English Journal*, Nov. 1999 (© 1999 NCTE)

Lyon, Hillary: "Jonathan, Asleep in Class"

Mali, Taylor: "The The Impotence of Proofreading," "Like Lilly Like Wilson," "Playing Scrabble with Eddie," "Undivided Attention," "What Teachers Make"; "Like Lilly Like Wilson" and "Playing Scrabble with Eddie" first appeared in *The Underwood Review*, Spring/Summer 1998; "What Teachers Make" first appeared in *Will Work for Peace* (Zeropanik 1999)

Maloy, Angela M.: "To Father" from *English Journal*, Nov. 1990 (© 1990 NCTE)

Martin, Deena L.: "Soliloquy" from *Reading Teacher*, Nov. 1999 (© *Reading Teacher* 1999; reprinted by permission)

Michaels, Judy: "Earth Day, 1999: Shootings at Columbine High," "Tasting the Word"; "April Inhalation," "For My Student Who Said, 'That's for Children,'" "October 12: Student Conference," and "October 22: Fourth Grade Classroom" © by Tom Thomson; reprinted by permission. The last four poems will appear in the *Forest of Wild Hands*, a collection to be printed by University Press of Florida

Morris, Cecil W.: "The Cowboy in English" from *English Journal*, Mar. 1995 (© 1995 NCTE), "Teaching Dreams" from *English Journal*, Sept. 1993 (© 1993 NCTE)

Nauss, Jenny: "The Long Answer"

Neelon, Ann: "Bulletin Board"

Oran, Sally M.: "Brian," "Cherokee Father/Son," "Desert Disciple," "Keys," "Moon-Chasing," "This Makes Me Strong," "Tightrope Walking at Fifty-Four"

Pagnac, Kelly Joe: "Mother"

Patton, Susan: "The Lesson," "With a Log Pencil"

Peck, Gail: "Half-Light" from *English Journal*, Jan. 1999 (© 1999 NCTE)

Pyle, John V.: "Thank You" from *English Journal*, Feb. 1983 (© 1983 NCTE)

Raines, Peggy: "Bygone Dreams," "Eric," "My Bones, My Life," "No Picnic," "Transformation"

Razler, Marion: "Pieces of a Country Childhood" first appeared in *English Journal*, May 1980

Reinart, Janie: "Marked for Life"

Reinsberg, Carol: "A Thank-You Note to My Student" from *English Journal*, Nov. 1983 (© 1983 NCTE)

Ruderman, Renee: "Weekend," "The Women with Accents"

Saenz, Sylvia: "Sara Smiled"

Shelley, Clarence: "Portrait #24" first appeared in *Collaborations*, Fall 1994

Snook, Eileen: "Opposites"

Spillane, Lee Ann: "Valerie"

Stansberger, Rick: "Autopsy Girl" from *English Journal*, Sept. 1995 (© 1995 NCTE)

St. Clair, Donald D.: "6 East, Line 100" from *English Journal*, Jan. 1992 (© 1992 NCTE)

Swanson, Nancy V.: "Sunday's Child" from *English Journal*, Apr. 1995 (© 1995 NCTE)

Thomas, Elizabeth: "For Father Cardenal," "From the Front of the Classroom," "I Don't Think So," "Revelation"; "For Father Cardenal" and "Revelation" first appeared in *Full Circle* (Hanover 2000)

Thornton, Thomas E.: "On Wiesel's *Night*" from *English Journal*, Feb. 1990 (© 1990 NCTE)

Trowbridge, Ruth: "Between the Lines" from *English Journal*, May 1975 (© 1975 NCTE)

Wagner, Maryfrances: "Chemotherapy," "Depth Finder," "Final Impressions," "Front of the Bus," "Giant Clown," "The Importance of Kneading," "Mask-Making in a Farmhouse Kitchen," "Mr. Cohick's Physical Science Class," "The Results of Some Hoping," "Salute"; "Chemotherapy" and "Mask-Making in a Farmhouse Kitchen" first appeared in *Kansas City Outloud II* (BkMk 1990); "Depth Finder" first appeared in *Potpourri*, Vol. 12., No. 2, 2000; "Final Impressions" first appeared in *Internet Zine* (Any Key 2000); "Mr. Cohick's Physical Science Class" first appeared in *Red Silk* (MidAmerica 1999); "Front of the Bus" first appeared in *Voices of Italian Americana*, Spring 2000; "Giant Clown" first appeared in *Midwest Women Writers*, *Sheba Review*, 1987; "The Importance of Kneading" first appeared in *New Letters*, Fall 1990; "The Results of Some Hoping" first appeared in *Laurel Review*, Vol. 32, No. 2, 1998; "Salute" first appeared in *Jam Today*, Vol. 15, 1990

Warman, Janet: "For English 200," "Teacher"; "For English 200" first appeared in *Colonnades*, 1992

Williams, Marty: "Andre Morgan's Fresh Rap," "The Dance," "Learning to Read"

Winston, William: "Question Unanswered"

Young, Roselyn: "Barbara at Forty-Five" from *English Journal*, Dec. 1993 (© 1993 NCTE); "For Barbara, On the Death of Her Student" from *English Journal*, Apr. 1983 (© 1983 NCTE)

Zobel, Diane Aro: "New Class" from *English Journal*, Nov. 1998 (© 1998 NCTE)

The volume editor and publisher have made every effort to include copyright and first publication information for the poems that appear in this book. Please contact the publisher with any additional information. ❧

INDEX OF CONTRIBUTORS AND POEMS

About the Author

Margaret Hatcher, Ed.D., has devoted her entire professional life to the field of education. She began her journey as a high-school English and creative-writing teacher and is now a university professor. Along her path as an educator, she has filled various leadership roles, including department chair, principal, and university dean. She currently serves on the faculty of the

Center for Excellence in Education at Northern Arizona University. Her interests in literature and art go beyond the academic; she is also a story-teller, published poet, and award-winning artist. She lives in Flagstaff, Arizona.

Renew Your Spirit with These Books from *Zephyr Press*

MINDSHIFTS (Second Edition)
A Brain-Compatible Process for Professional Growth and the Renewal of Education
by Geoffrey Caine, LL.M., Renate Nummela Caine, Ph.D., and Sam Crowell, Ed.D.

Professional Growth   ISBN: 1-56976-091-8

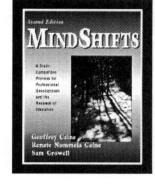

This landmark book has been revised and updated with the best, latest information from brain research and teacher feedback. You'll have a road map for staff development and school change that clarifies the personal and system changes that schools need to make for success in the 21st century. Use it as the focus of your training or to synthesize other techniques and strategies. Look to *MindShifts* for a self- and school-discovery process that nets outstanding professional results!
1150-W . . . $37.00

THE RE-ENCHANTMENT OF LEARNING
A Manual for Teacher Renewal and Classroom Transformation
by Sam Crowell, Ed.D., Renate Nummela Caine, Ph.D., and Geoffrey Caine, LL.M.

Professional Growth   ISBN: 1-56976-076-4

Optimize learning and realize human potential with this step-by-step guide. *The Re-Enchantment of Learning* takes you through a ten-week process. Each chapter begins with information and inspiration to give you a foundation for the activities at the end.

Boost your effectiveness in meeting today's challenges with strategies based on the new sciences. Applications of these field-tested methods have resulted in higher student grades and test scores. And more importantly, dramatic transformations are evidenced by personal lives taking on a renewed sense of meaning, administrators focusing on bringing out the best in everyone, and students taking pride in their work.
1082-W . . . $32.00

TEACHING IN THE TAO
by Patrick Christie

Professional Growth   ISBN: 1-56976-126-4

Like the *Tao Te Ching,* the ancient Chinese text, *Teaching in the Tao* provides teachers with philosophical expressions of harmony and compassion to help them in their chosen "way" of teaching. All teachers will relate with the realities presented in this book. Christie's thoughts will inspire you to remember why you chose teaching as a profession in the first place. Each of the short chapters is a poetic reflection of interest to educators.
1124-W . . . $11.95

Renew Your Spirit with These Books from *Zephyr Press*

3 CHEERS FOR TEACHING!
A Guide to Growing Professionally and Renewing Your Spirit
by Bonita DeAmicis
Professional Growth   ISBN: 1-56976-094-2

Become the teacher you know you can be with these effective strategies for making real change in your life and work. Exercises and activities show you how to turn ideas and dreams into actions and results. *3 Cheers for Teaching!* is an extraordinary step-by-step program that will help you uncover what you need to know in order to teach well. If you've been looking for an easy way to initiate your own professional growth plan, this simple yet transforming three-part program makes right now the perfect time to get started.
1098-W . . . $27.00

TEACHER, TEACH ON! poster set
Professional Growth   1-56976-132-9
Draw daily inspiration from these charming posters. Quotes from Bonita DeAmicis's *3 Cheers for Teaching! A Guide to Growing Professionally and Renewing Your Spirit* do just that—lift the spirits. Treat yourself to these gems for visual enjoyment and to re-charge your spirit. Use them all together in the teachers' lounge or display one at a time. The visual appeal and strong words of encouragement are sure to be appreciated.

8 full-color, 11" x 17" posters
1824-W . . . $27.00

Qty.	Item #	Title	Unit Price	Total

Name _____

Address _____

City _____

State _____ Zip _____

Phone (_____) _____

E-mail _____

Subtotal	
Sales Tax (AZ residents, 5.6%)	
S & H (10% of Subtotal, min. $5.50)	
Total (U.S. Funds only)	

CANADA: add 30% for S& H and G.S.T.

Method of payment (check one):

❑ Check or Money Order ❑ Visa

❑ MasterCard ❑ Purchase Order Attached

Credit Card No. _____

Expires _____

Signature _____

Extraordinary Classroom Materials for Extraordinary K–12 Teachers

Call, write, e-mail, or FAX for your FREE catalog!

P.O. Box 66006-W
Tucson, AZ 85728-6006
520-322-5090
1-800-232-2187
FAX 520-323-9402
www.zephyrpress.com
www.i-home-school.com
neways2learn@zephyrpress.com

Zephyr Press